MW00945727

Steps Forward

The New Adventures of Ernest Thorpe

Michael W. Newman

Dedication

To Cindy, who brought me to the little blue cottage where Ernest Thorpe came to life;

To Hannah and Abby, who listened to the stories I told;

To mom and dad, who let my imagination run wild;

To Grandma and Grandpa Krentz, who welcomed me to their little Shangri-La with open arms; and

To the people of Prince of Peace, who allowed Ernest to bring them truths from God's Word on many Sundays.

Contents

How to use *Steps Forward*

I hope you enjoy these stories of Ernest Thorpe and his friends. Your goal may be to read, enjoy, and be edified. That's okay.

I would like to suggest, however, that you think about using this book to take advantage of the power of what a story can do in the lives of the people around you. Stories do something special. They make you think. They draw you into an experience and surprise you. They catch you off guard and change your outlook.

My challenge to you would be to share these stories. Read them with your spouse or with a friend. Read them to your children or grandchildren. Use the Devotion/Study Guide at the end of each chapter to think and talk and pray about what God is doing in your heart and how He is directing you in life.

When the story of God's grace works its way into your life, you'll be delighted. In a world that holds you back and sends you on wild goose chases, you'll be doing something different. You'll be taking STEPS FORWARD!

Thanks for reading,

Michael W. Newman

Holding Onto God
Steps Forward
Chapter One

Jesus said, "Watch out! Be on guard against being compelled toward more and more..." Luke 12:15

Ernest Thorpe threw up. I know that is a terrible way to begin a book, but facts are facts. Ernest threw up. He didn't expect it and he was a little embarrassed, but after running full tilt for two miles Ernest's insides just didn't want to stay inside. Fortunately he was outside. Ernest wiped his mouth with the back of his hand, and his hand on the side of his running shorts. Still bent over he could see a pair of worn running shoes step up next to him.

"Way to go, Ernest," said the voice. "You looked good in that tryout. You beat them all."

Ernest looked up. It was Manny Andrews. Manny Andrews was a former Harrison High School runner. It would be more accurate to say that Manny Andrews was a Harrison legend. He set records as a Harrison Hornet runner. He was 37 years old— an old man according to Ernest. Manny was the one setting the pace for the High School runners at the spring track tryout. Ernest beat everyone in that track tryout race except the old man, Manny Andrews. Ernest straightened up and grudgingly shook Manny Andrews' hand.

"Thanks," Ernest said.

Manny pointed to Ernest's chin. Ernest quickly wiped away a few drips that he missed. Then Manny and Ernest went their separate ways.

Losing to an old man, throwing up in front of him, and having a mess on your chin—how embarrassing! It was humiliating! Ernest vowed that it would never happen again—especially the losing part.

Ernest planned on winning that race. And he did—almost. But almost wasn't good enough. That may be what pushed Ernest into high gear as he entered the track season. He did not want to be denied, so he raced with a vengeance.

Something new had awakened inside Ernest. Here was a boy who, just a short time ago, wasn't motivated to clean his room. There were times he was too lazy even to press the buttons on the remote control when he was watching television. He didn't feel very enthusiastic about going along on outings with his family. Sleeping in whenever he could had become a pastime in his life. But now something had changed. He felt driven. He wanted to win—more than that, he was starting to shape his life around winning. A deeply competitive nature was growing inside him. Being the best was becoming his nature—at least the best in running.

During the track season Ernest won some middle distance events. He even got his picture in the local weekly newspaper, the Clare County Cleaver. The season was becoming a success for the new track runner Ernest Thorpe. And the success fueled the desire for more. More success. More competition. More training. More achievement. Ernest was feeling good about running and about himself. He also felt that reaching his ultimate goal was possible: cross country tryouts in the fall. Fellow students would not be the only ones running that race. Manny Andrews would be there too. And Ernest Thorpe wanted to beat Manny Andrews.

The track season ended well for Ernest. His confidence was at a high point. His track coach praised him and encouraged him to keep working hard over the summer. Ernest thanked the coach and said, "I will."

Ernest had a plan. First he bought new running shoes—the latest in running footwear. Ernest spent most of what he saved through the year, but it didn't matter. He was going all out. Ernest spent hours devising a summer workout schedule that would ensure him success against his nemesis. Two workouts each day would be the standard for the summer. Then there was fuel—that's what he was calling food lately. Ernest streamlined his diet for running efficiency. He skipped many of the meals his mom prepared and substituted a balance of carbohydrates and proteins that would maximize his running potential. He asked the owner of the Harrison Rexall Drug Store to order Power Bars so he could refuel while he was running. Ernest Thorpe became a running machine.

Life became different for the Thorpe family. This running machine, their son, was creating havoc at home. Ernest insisted on going to church sweaty because his workout schedule called for precision timing. There was no time to shower between running and church. That went over big with his sister and brother who had to share the back seat with him. Ernest even missed his little brother's one-year birthday party because of a scheduled workout.

"If you're going to go for it, you've got to go for it all the way," Ernest told his mom.

And Ernest did. He went for it to the point of interrupting the course of his life. His parents could see that his life had become one-dimensional. But a one-dimensional life doesn't only affect the person living it. It affects everyone around him. And it was doing just that. But Ernest couldn't stop. It was as if he was compelled toward more and more. Beating Manny Andrews had become what life was all about. It would make him happy. It would mean satisfaction. It would make his life complete—at least that's what this sophomore thought.

Isn't it amazing how something so healthy and good could become so unhealthy and destructive? But this was new territory for Ernest. He had never experienced this kind of success and recognition. He had never felt this drive.

The Saturday night after James' one-year birthday party Ernest got a phone call. It was from the old man—Manny Andrews. Ernest was nervous as he picked up the phone. Could he fraternize with the enemy? Would this weaken him psychologically?

Ernest said, "Hello?"

Manny asked Ernest if they could work out. Together. Tomorrow morning.

Ernest was shocked. Work out? Run together? How would this fit into his plan? Ernest had to think quickly. Maybe this would fit into his plan perfectly. Pump the old man for information. Find out how fast he could really run. Lay back a little bit and make it look like he's getting out of shape over the summer. Get Manny overconfident. Then when fall came Manny would be the one falling into Ernest's trap! Ernest couldn't say no.

Sunday morning, early, there was a knock at the door. Ernest was dressed, stretched and ready. He opened the door to see Manny Andrews standing there...in HIS CHURCH CLOTHES! Church clothes?! Manny asked Ernest to sit down. The legend and the sophomore sat side by side on the front stoop.

"Ernest, Manny said, "I understand that your life has been interrupted a little bit."

Was this a trick? Ernest was giving away nothing. "No," Ernest replied, "What do you mean?"

Manny answered, "Ernest, what have you been living and breathing so far during summer vacation?"

"Well, I've been working out a little bit." Ernest gave as little information as possible.

Manny continued. "I like running, Ernest. In fact, I love it. I used to be a running fool. I have all kinds of records at the high school—you know that."

Ernest wondered if Manny was trying to psych him out.

"But Ernest," Manny said, "Success, while a great blessing, can be very dangerous. You can get hooked on it. It can become your life. You can start to live for the next thing, the next win, the next competition, the next goal. You think you'll finally get to the point of being satisfied at the top. But Ernest, there is no top."

> *"I found out that all the running in the world, all the things I thought I wanted, didn't take me one step forward."*

Then Manny asked, "Do you know why I'm not married?"

Ernest shook his head no.

"Because I lost the girl I loved doing what you're doing," Manny said.

He continued: "Ernest, I tried chasing after more for too many years after high school. And I found out that all the running in the world, all the things I thought I wanted, didn't take me one step forward. Understand me, now. I'm not trying to tell you to stop running. I'm just trying to tell you to stop chasing. Life doesn't come from what you chase down in life. It comes from who chased you down."

There was Manny Andrews in church clothes telling Ernest about Jesus.

Manny said, "If you want some steps forward, let Jesus be in charge of the race."

Ernest asked Manny Andrews, "Who told you about what I was doing?"

Manny replied, "Let's just say I heard that a little boy named James really missed you at his first birthday, okay?"

Manny went on, "So get your church clothes on, Ernest. If we're going to race, we're going to start at the right place."

Ernest did what Manny asked. He changed—his clothes and his attitude. And off they went, a running legend and a beginner. That morning Ernest realized that what made Manny such a great runner, such a success, is that he knew how to run more than just a foot race. This was the beginning of something new—new friendship, and new insight into life. The competitive juices were still flowing in Ernest Thorpe, but now life was beginning to grow alongside the adrenaline that continued to flow. Manny Andrews helped Ernest get his life in position. He was learning to be in the right place so he could participate in all of life. Manny described it as real life, Christ-life.

And even when Manny Andrews beat Ernest again at the fall cross country tryouts, Ernest knew that he was still taking steps forward.

"Let us run with perseverance the race marked out for us, fixing our eyes on Jesus, the author and perfecter of our faith…"

Devotion/Study Guide for chapter 1: Steps Forward

Discuss:

Read Luke 12:15-20

What areas of life are sending you chasing lately?

How does the advice that Manny Andrews gave Ernest impact you?

Read Hebrews 12:1-3

How does Jesus provide a balance for you in life?

What encouragement do you receive from the verses in Hebrews 12?

Apply:

Read Luke 12:31-32

List three priorities in life that God wants you to give your attention to. Evaluate whether or not you are giving time and attention to these areas.

Pray:

Thank God for chasing you down and reclaiming your life in Jesus. Ask God to lead you to lead a balanced life. Mention areas of your life that need a more healthy balance.

Heads Up
Chapter Two

———————————

"Stand up and lift up your heads, because your redemption is drawing near." Luke 21:28

Mrs. Thorpe could not find the crayons. They had to be there! It was back to school time. She had the sale flyer in hand. She was at the store early enough. But where were they? Pens, markers, erasers, pencils—everything was in clear view. Except the crayons! Finally a salesperson came by.

"Where are the crayons?" Mrs. Thorpe asked. "I can't find the crayons!"

She was exasperated. The salesperson could tell. Mrs. Thorpe could tell the salesperson could tell.

"Ma'am," the kind young man began. "Do you see that large display to your right? The one with the big red crayon sign that says 'Crayon Clearout'? They're right there."

Mrs. Thorpe felt the embarrassment immediately. "Thank you," she answered in a calm and apologetic tone.

What was going on? Was it age? Was it too much to do? Why could she not see what was right in front of her?

Mrs. Thorpe felt frazzled. In Harrison it was that time of year. It was back to school preparation time. Ernest Thorpe was getting ready for his sophomore year in High School. His little sister Karen would be starting second grade. In the midst of the busyness and preparation, Mr. and Mrs. Thorpe wanted one last getaway before the school schedule started. One last weekend of relaxation sounded like the relief they needed. So they planned a four day trip to a cabin in the upper peninsula of Michigan. It was in an isolated location, situated on some bluffs that overlooked Lake Michigan. In the brochure for the cabin there were words like "serenity" and "peace" and "refreshment." The pictures showed majestic sunsets and beautiful wildlife. It looked like a perfect spot. But first, preparation for school and the trip had to happen.

Mrs. Thorpe purchased all the required school supplies—crayons included. She bought new shoes for everyone, went to the grade school and high school registrations, met the children's teachers, made a doctor appointment for Ernest's sports physical, and set up a one year appointment for James at the same time. Mr. Thorpe had to take the truck in for some unexpected transmission work. Ernest was going to cut the grass. Mrs. Thorpe was going to pack. All of the activity made Mrs. Thorpe wonder if the getaway was worthwhile, but that brochure kept convincing her. They just had to get away. So, the preparation continued.

Mr. Thorpe was elected to take Ernest and James to the doctor. Ernest checked out okay. James was in top condition, a healthy and growing one-year-old. But the doctor said to Mr. Thorpe, "I've been looking at that mole on your neck. I think you should have that looked at. Let me get you an appointment with a good dermatologist I know."

That was a surprise, but Mr. Thorpe was able to go to the doctor in Clare the next day. The dermatologist took a look and told Mr. Thorpe that he would have to consult a surgeon. There appeared to be a small mass underneath the mole. The doctor indicated that it probably would have to be removed. The office set up an appointment with the surgeon for later in the afternoon. This doctor confirmed that a mass was there and that it would be best if the mass was removed for a biopsy. By this time Mrs. Thorpe had driven down to Clare to be with her husband. Ernest was watching Karen and James. Mr. and Mrs. Thorpe agreed on this course of action. The surgery was planned for Thursday morning. It would be an outpatient procedure.

All of this was happening very quickly. Each doctor treated each step with cool professionalism. It all seemed routine—to them! But as the doctors talked about surgical procedures, pathology reports, and the chances of malignancy, Mr. Thorpe was getting shaken up. He prided himself in being a pretty tough guy, but he had never been through this before. He knew people who died from skin cancer. He read plenty of articles about it. Less than forty-eight hours ago Mr. Thorpe was focused on preparation for the school year and a weekend trip. Now he had thoughts about life and death. To be honest, it was frightening. The unanswered questions and myriad of worries coursed through Mr. Thorpe's mind. His life, his family, the future—what would happen? One voice in his head kept asking the questions: Would he die a painful death? Did he have enough insurance? What would his funeral be like? Would his kids be okay? Would his wife remarry? Another voice urged him to slow down, to take one step at a time, and to pray. That's what he did.

Mr. Thorpe arrived at the outpatient center in Clare early Thursday morning. He filled out the necessary forms. He was given a hospital gown to put on. And there he was. He was with several other patients waiting for their turn. Music played on the speaker over head. "We will never pass this way again" the lyrics said. People seemed to be very casual about all this. They read newspapers and magazines. Mr. Thorpe thought about the surgery. The variety of possible outcomes started coursing through his mind again. He thought about the possibility of cancer. Oh, but this was just a biopsy. No sense in getting worked up over nothing. Everything would probably be just fine. But, what if...? What a strange situation he was in, Mr. Thorpe thought to himself. He was afraid about his life, but life just kept going. The weather was on the radio now. Magazine pages turned in the waiting room. Passersby talked and laughed in the hallway. Mr. Thorpe asked his wife to pray with him. They held hands, bowed their heads, and whispered words to God. They asked for help and peace and good results and strength.

The praying never really stopped. Even when Mr. Thorpe went in for surgery, both of the Thorpe's kept praying. It was a silent dialog with the Great Physician.

The surgery went well. The doctor encouraged Mr. Thorpe to take the weekend getaway with his family. He might as well relax. The biopsy results would be ready Monday. The doctor apologized for the weekend delay, but he said Mr. Thorpe could call the office first thing Monday.

So, off the Thorpe family went. Mr. Thorpe felt good. He even drove the last part of the trip. And the cabin was great! It was better than the brochure described. There was a beautiful view of Lake Michigan and some islands in the distance. It was quiet. And they were together.

After the kids went to bed, Mr. and Mrs. Thorpe sat outside. They listened to the lake send its waves onto the rocky shore. Mr. Thorpe said to his wife, "I hope everything is okay." Mrs. Thorpe agreed. "The Lord will take care of you," she said. "Of us," she added.

Mr. Thorpe had a lot on his mind. "It's like being in two worlds," he said. "You do your normal things, but you think about life and death too."

> *"All the things to get and to do in life can really take my eyes off what's important."*

Mr. Thorpe looked up at the stars in the sky. He sat with his arm around his wife. He kept talking: "When is the last time we looked at the stars? I can't even remember the last time I actually saw them!"

Mrs. Thorpe agreed.

"All the things to get and to do in life can really take my eyes off what's important," Mr. Thorpe reflected.

Mrs. Thorpe was glad to hear her husband talk like that. They sat for a while and looked at the stars.

On Sunday morning, the Thorpe family had a morning family devotion on the bluff. The sun was rising. They were surrounded by trees and water. It was a beautiful setting for the worship of God. Mr. Thorpe read the words of Jesus: *"Do not be afraid, little flock, for your Father has been pleased to give you the kingdom. Sell your possessions and give to the poor. Provide purses for yourselves that will not wear out, a treasure in heaven that will not be exhausted, where no thief comes near and no moth destroys. For where your treasure is, there your heart will be also" (Luke 12:32-34).* Mr. Thorpe talked about what was on all their minds. "I'm sure I'll be okay," he said. "I'm praying I'll be okay. Jesus says, 'Don't be afraid.' He died on the cross for me. He forgave me. I'm blessed now and I've got heaven forever. That's the best treasure to depend on. It's what really counts."

Mr. Thorpe looked at his family. "And I'm glad we share that treasure."

After singing "Jesus Loves Me" and praying the Lord's Prayer, the family enjoyed the rest of the day together.

Monday morning came, and Mr. Thorpe had no trouble getting out of bed. He drove to a gas station about fifteen miles away where he could make the phone call. He dialed the number. Mr. Thorpe's heart pounded. The nurse answered and put Mr. Thorpe through to the doctor. It seemed to take forever. The gas station attendant watched Mr. Thorpe. Mr. Thorpe waited for the doctor and prayed. Finally the doctor came on the line.

"I've got good news for you," he said. "It's all clear. The mass was benign. Everything looked good. You'll be fine."

Mr. Thorpe hung up the phone. He turned and looked at the road, the trees, everything around him. It all looked brand new. He prayed a prayer of thanks to his Savior. As Mr. Thorpe started to walk away from the phone, another gas station worker called out, "Heads up!" The attendant had to drive past Mr. Thorpe to get his tow truck into the garage.

"Heads up," Mr. Thorpe said. "More than you know, friend."

He got into his truck to go share the good news with his family.

Yes, the Thorpe family headed back home from their northern Michigan getaway. No, it wasn't back to life as usual again. It wasn't just back to the routine, eyes drawn to all the needs, the cares, the news, and the things to do in life. For the thankful Thorpe family, as the long weekend came to an end, they were beginning the busy fall season with HEADS UP—eyes on what really matters in life, heart rooted in the treasure of the promise and care of Jesus. Heads up. It was good to be brought that way again.

Devotion/Study Guide for chapter 2: Heads Up

Discuss:

Read Psalm 121:1-8

What have you been getting distracted by lately?

Have you ever been through a life-perspective changing experience like Mr. Thorpe?

How did it make you feel? Did it change your outlook?

What promise does God give you as you face difficult times?

Apply:

Talk about two or three ways you can live a "heads up" life in the week ahead.

Pray:

Thank God for being the Helper you can look to. Ask God to help you with one challenge in your life. Let God know one fear you have. Ask Him to see you through it.

Holding Onto God
Hands In
Chapter Three

———————

"O Lord... you have laid your hand upon me. If I rise on the wings of the dawn, if I settle on the far side of the sea, even there your hand will guide me, your right hand will hold me fast."

Psalm 139:4b, 5b, 9-10

A s the sun sets and the shadows grow long over Budd Lake, through the warm summer air in Harrison, a peculiar sound echoes across the landscape: Slap! Mosquitoes. That is, people attempting to defend themselves against mosquitoes. Summer is a time when the tourist population and the mosquito population grow in Harrison. And whenever the mosquito population grows, a question that has been asked through all of time comes up: "Why did God make mosquitoes anyway?"

That kind of question makes you wonder where God is in the middle of this big world and this very complex life that just keeps on going. But that's what happens. They just keep going. And that is how life was in Harrison—it just kept going.

First there was the news about Aunt Val. She was one of Mr. Thorpe's sisters. She just turned forty. Aunt Val phoned to say that she was getting married! For all these years Val thought that the right man just wasn't out there. She made up her mind that she would remain an independent single woman. But that is when God surprised her. Val happened to meet a wonderful Christian man in her office building. It didn't take long for either of them to know that they were right for each other. The rest was history. Now they had plans for an early October wedding. What great news to hear! Mrs. Thorpe put the big event on the calendar and wrote a note about buying a gift and a card. It was a good addition to life that kept going.

Exciting things were happening at home too. Little James, the youngest of the three Thorpe children and now one year old, was making his way around the house on two feet. He was walking! In fact, there was no part of the house he didn't want to walk around in. This caused Ernest to take some defensive measures. Ernest, now a sophomore in high school, made sure his bedroom door was closed. He saw how James was infatuated with playing with the water in the toilet. Even though Mrs. Thorpe did all she could to prevent James' splashing adventures in the bathroom, Ernest didn't want to let anyone with that mind-set into his room!

James' enthusiasm for his new talent of walking caused some new adventures at home. He could be downright dangerous. Mr. and Mrs. Thorpe were sure that several of God's angels were surrounding James as he took all kinds of tumbles and missed sharp corners by inches. Life certainly kept going in the Thorpe household!

Karen, now in second grade, was not as enthusiastic about her environment. She had a new teacher, a new classroom—new everything it seemed! And she was one nervous little girl at the start of another school year. Mornings began with tears or nervous laughter. Only a big hug and kiss along with a special prayer to

Jesus could get Karen to open the car door and head into school in the morning. It was a difficult thing, but life keeps going, and sometimes you need a nudge to keep going with it.

Ernest Thorpe's scenario was a little more stressful than that of James and Karen. Maybe it was because Mr. and Mrs. Thorpe felt they had less control over their high school son. Some of Ernest's friends were driving, and it wouldn't be long before he would get his driver's permit. Inspired by their new-found freedom, a few of Ernest's friends planned an innocent outing. They were going to drive to Detroit! If that wasn't enough to increase the gray hair count of any Harrison parent, Ernest and his friends wanted to go to the Motor City so they could take in a rock concert! Detroit and a rock concert. Mr. and Mrs. Thorpe never imagined that they would reach this stage of parenting. Detroit, a rock concert, and their fifteen-year-old son. Those didn't add up, and it wasn't going to happen! Mr. and Mrs. Thorpe intervened quickly and put an end to any idea of a road trip for Ernest. It turned out that all of the boys found themselves in the position of lamenting their fate together. Not one of the parents would go for that excursion. Life keeps going, but sometimes you can keep it from going into places that are a little too wild.

Pastor Graff, the faithful pastor of St. Luke Lutheran Church in Harrison, also saw that life kept going. He had a unique vantage point when it came to observing life. A pastor lives through the highs and lows of the people around him. He's there to weep with the broken-hearted and to rejoice with those who are celebrating. He listens intently to people who need to talk about serious issues, and he laughs at the latest joke that a member of his church wants to share. Sometimes this roller coaster ride can be overwhelming—even numbing. In the morning parents celebrate the baptism of the child they desperately prayed to have. In the afternoon a family gathers in tears as they grieve the death of a husband and father who died much too soon. At one moment a pastor prays with someone who is tired of illness and suffering and is asking Jesus to come and take her home. At another moment a pastor is giving direction to a person who is excited about finding a new course of action to use his gifts and serve God with all his heart. Ups and downs. Highs and lows. At the end of the day, how should you feel? God's blessing and God's silence. There were many times that Pastor Graff wondered where God was in the middle of this life that just keeps on going. Pastor Graff knew that a lot of other people were wondering the same thing. He saw this issue make and break people's faith. This was serious. It became a matter of life and death.

> *Ups and downs. Highs and lows. At the end of the day, how should you feel?*

It was during a time that Pastor Graff was feeling particularly numb, drained, confused, and burned out, that God brought him an answer about where He was in the middle of life that kept on going. The answer came in the form of a lady named Maryann Peak. Pastor Graff stopped in to see her while she was hospitalized. Maryann was over ninety-years-old. She was facing some pretty challenging health issues, but as she talked to Pastor Graff he could feel life being breathed back into him again. God had something to say to him, and he wanted to hear it. So he listened to Maryann.

As she lay in her hospital bed, she spoke in a quiet voice. She was weak, but her eyes were bright—clear blue, and her slight southern accent, an accent that traced her roots, added a beautiful lilt to every word.

"The Lord knows the way through the wilderness," She began. "He'll lead us. With Jesus by my side I'll be just fine."

Pastor Graff brought communion, and Maryann commented, "As I look at my life, I know there are times I let the Lord down. But He cast my sin in the depths of the sea and put up a 'No Fishing' sign. When I look at my life I see God, active and blessing me every day."

Suddenly Pastor Graff saw life with amazing clarity. Here was a woman who gave up her home and all her possessions. She lived in a nursing home that was not the best in giving attention or help. She struggled with health problems that took away her ability to walk or read or knit or even sit upright for extended periods of time. And yet she said, "When I look at my life I see God, active and blessing me every day." Maryann could see where God was in the middle of this life that keeps on going. God was right there. Present. With her every moment. He had His hands in her life, even if life was not going the way she preferred.

Here was wisdom and perspective that needed to be shared. So "Blessing Sunday" was born. On the weekend after he visited Maryann, Pastor Graff announced to his congregation that the following Sunday was going to be a special celebration. It would be "Blessing Sunday." People would be asked to share how they have seen God in their lives. Anyone interested could contact Pastor Graff during the week. They would then be invited to talk briefly in next Sunday's service about the Lord's work in their life. Pastor Graff was convinced that people needed a time to locate God again. The course of life crowds God out. It makes you wonder if He is real or present, or if He even cares. It was time to let people speak up. It was time to let God's hand be seen.

That Sunday Pastor Graff started off by reading from the Bible. He said to the people gathered that day, "God promised to keep His hands in your lives. Because of His love He doesn't give up on you. He cares and He works."

Then Pastor Graff read from Jeremiah 23: *"'Am I only a God nearby, and not a God far away? Can anyone hide in the secret places so that I cannot see him? Do I not fill heaven and earth?' declares the Lord" (Jeremiah 23:23-29).*

Pastor Graff said to his gathered flock, "With all the ups and downs in life, it's easy to think that God is either in just a few places, or not around at all. The Bible says that God hasn't abandoned us, that He is with us every step of the way. But I don't want to be the one who has to convince you. Listen for yourself."

Then a beautiful thing happened. A husband and wife stood up and talked about how their marriage was healed and was growing again because of the love of Christ that touched their lives through some caring friends.

A widow stood up and, with tears, talked about the blessing of her husband's life in heaven. She would see him again.

A man in his forties said he was blessed when he was in an accident and received a fine for driving drunk. It was a turning point as he admitted his alcoholism and was on the road to recovery.

Another man—fairly new to St. Luke—talked about how his open heart surgery and a Christian neighbor brought the blessing of God into his life. He was going it alone until he saw that he couldn't make it by himself. That heart scare was a blessing, he said.

A little girl got up and said that her new puppy was a blessing.

A Sunday School teacher talked about the blessing of the children she taught.

A member of the church said that the blessing of the people in the congregation was special in his life.

A mom said that she is more able to cope with all the demands of life because of Jesus' care and His Word of encouragement.

Blessing Sunday. Everyone wasn't eloquent. The words didn't bear testimony to mountains that were moved, or to miraculous healings. But every word did bear testimony to the miracle of a God who is very close, very present, and very active in life that keeps on going.

Mr. and Mrs. Thorpe were among the people at church that day who were truly encouraged. Their eyes were placed on Jesus again. As their lives kept on going, they knew that there was a reason not to grow weary and lose heart. God was there, active and blessing them every day. Sometimes that's hard to see. That's why it helps to take a peek through someone else's eyes once in a while.

As the Thorpe family headed home that Sunday morning, they had a new perspective. Whether it was the surprise of a husband for Aunt Val, divine protection for James, a prayer for peace for Karen, or stepping in with some firm action for Ernest; whether it was through all the stress and strain that money or job or family or people or life brings; God has His hands in.

Devotion/Study Guide for chapter 3: Hands In

Discuss:

Read Psalm 139:1-12

When do you doubt God's presence in your life?

What causes you to wonder if He is active in this world?

How do the verses from Psalm 139 speak to those doubts?

How do the events of "blessing Sunday" help answer your questions and doubts?

Apply:

Have your own blessing day. As an individual or family, mention two or three ways you see and have seen God at work in your life.

Pray:

Ask God about your doubts or questions. Let Him know that you'll be watching for His answers. Thank God for the blessings you mentioned or thought about.

Handling Life's Hardships
One Way
Chapter Four

———————

"Come, let us go up to the mountain of the LORD, to the house of the God of Jacob. He will teach us his ways, so that we may walk in his paths." Isaiah 2:3

I f you've never seen the big, wet snowflakes that blow into Harrison, you just haven't seen snow. Sometimes it looks like all the kids in town cut fancy snowflakes out of white paper and set them loose just as a north winter breeze began to blow. The month of December is a special time in the "Playground of the North." Harrison gets ready for all kinds of snowy recreation. Unfortunately, the snow was slow in coming this year. The grass was still visible and the temperatures were too balmy for the snow recreation enthusiasts. Karen Thorpe, the seven-year-old daughter of Mr. and Mrs. Thorpe, decided to use the warm weather for some wiffle ball practice. Her dad was trying to interest her in some sports and wiffle ball turned out to be a popular outdoor activity. Karen stood in the front yard with the determination of "Casey at the bat." As she tossed the ball into the air she said, "I'm the greatest baseball player in the world!" Then she would swing— and miss. Up the ball would go. A swing and a miss. "I'm the greatest player ever," she would say. Then a swing and a miss. "The best player there is!" Then a mighty swing and no contact. "Wow!" Karen finally said, "What a pitcher I am!"

Sometimes it just depends on the way you look at what's happening. There were many perspectives to one big event that was happening in the Thorpe household. Ernest Thorpe was learning to drive. Ernest thought this was one of the more significant events in history. There was nothing more important than the pursuit of his driver's license. Ernest's mother had a bit of a different reaction. Behind her calm smile there was COMPLETE FEAR.

But Ernest's father was favorably inclined toward this landmark event in his son's life. Mr. Thorpe was glad that Ernest would be able to help out with some of the chauffeuring and errand running in their busy household. Mr. Thorpe's actions backed up his attitude. Every weekday he got up at 5:30 in the morning to drive Ernest to driver's education class.

Ernest got out of bed at the same time. The alarm went off and Ernest sprung out of bed to get ready. Driver's education classes were with Mr. Carr at Harrison High School—it was one of those names! The classes had to be squeezed in either before or after school. Ernest chose the former so he could get a jump on everyone else.

Mr. Thorpe was amazed to see his sophomore son up that early. He was actually communicating and ready to do something somewhat constructive. "This can't be all bad," Mr. Thorpe said to his wife as he tried to console her.

Mr. Thorpe's perspective did change a bit, however. When Ernest got his driver's permit he begged to pull the car out of the garage in the morning and to drive to school while his dad supervised from the passenger seat. What harm could there be in that? Good experience for the boy, Mr. Thorpe thought. And it was good experience. People say you learn from your mistakes. You see, Ernest was sure that the car was in PARK after he started it up and pulled it out of the garage. When he pressed the button to close the garage door, he was certain that the car wasn't going anywhere. No one actually witnessed the car backing into the garage door as it came down. The crash, however, was heard. That loud scraping and the snapping of wood panels is not a typical 6:00 a.m. sound.

Yes, the car was actually in reverse. Yes, Mrs. Thorpe reminded her husband that this was "good experience for the boy." This event must have shaken Ernest up a little bit. On the way to school he turned down a ONE WAY street—the wrong way. Fortunately, traffic was light at that early hour. The newspaper delivery man was the only person run off the road.

> *"There are a lot of different possibilities when you're on the road," Mr. Thorpe said to Ernest, "but there really is just ONE WAY to drive."*

After these learning experiences, Mr. Thorpe decided to do a little more "hands on" training. "There are a lot of different possibilities when you're on the road," Mr. Thorpe said to Ernest, "but there really is just ONE WAY to drive." Ernest's dad took him to the parking lot at the fairgrounds for a little safe practice time. Mr. Thorpe wanted to show Ernest the way.

The next step in Driver's Education was Behind the Wheel classes. The alarm went off every morning at 5:30 and Ernest was out of bed and ready to go. Since the garage door incident, Karen took cover in her bedroom. She told Ernest that she kept having nightmares about the house falling down.

Behind the wheel was great—even though Ernest had to take the class with a girl. Her name was Lisa Dale. She was nice enough, but her dad was a different story. Every day her dad would complain about something to Mr. Carr. Mr. Dale was loud and sounded pretty mean as he demanded these pre-class conversations. Ernest could tell that Mr. Carr dreaded these encounters more than anyone. But he was polite, calm, and a good listener. That's probably why he was a good driving teacher, too.

When the weekend came there was a break in this new driving adventure for the Thorpe's. Mrs. Thorpe made sure that a cease-driving time was implemented and stayed in effect through Saturday and Sunday. She was not ready to have her son drive her to church. Ernest had to settle for the back seat when mom was along.

It was December, and, even though the snow hadn't appeared, there were signs of the Christmas countdown all over town. That included St. Luke Lutheran Church. It was Advent, and the church looked beautiful. In his sermon Pastor Graff asked the people gathered for church that Sunday about the way they were going to go through this Advent season. "There are many ways to go," Pastor Graff said. He mentioned the stress that hits hard in the pre-Christmas rush. He talked about worry with all the arrangements and the financial strain that can take place. He talked about sadness. For a few members of St. Luke this would be the first Christmas without ones they loved. Ernest thought of Grandpa Thorpe. It would be the first Christmas without him.

Ernest saw his dad wipe away a tear. Pastor Graff talked about anger. Tempers can grow short in a season when so much is going on.

But instead of leaving us with question marks about the way to go, Pastor Graff noted, God is faithful. Instead of us handling the stress or worry, the sadness or anger, all alone, the Lord steps in and takes us His way. Pastor Graff quoted Isaiah chapter two: *"Come, let us go up to the mountain of the Lord, to the house of the God of Jacob. He will teach us His ways, so that we may walk in his paths...Come...let us walk in the light of the Lord."*

To Ernest it sounded like God was a good driving teacher—just like Mr. Carr. No matter what complaints, blame, anger, or opposition come along, God stays true. No matter how many mishaps and goof-ups take place, God stays true. He sent His Son. The gift of forgiveness and new life with Jesus mean that there is a wonderful way to go through Advent and through all of life. This was an important driving lesson for Ernest and for everyone listening.

"For work, for shopping, and for your family, there are a lot of different possibilities when you're on the road of life," Pastor Graff said. "But there really is just ONE WAY to go. What better way than through it all with Jesus Christ and the life He gives?"

On the way home from church Ernest saw the ONE WAY sign that he missed last week. When he saw it, he thought of more than just driving.

The next day Ernest was up bright and early again—awake from his slumber at 5:30 a.m. He made it to driver's ed. class. As

39

Ernest approached the car for behind the wheel training, he heard Mr. Dale yelling at Mr. Carr—something about the grading system and the school administration. Lisa looked sad and embarrassed. Ernest felt sad for her.

There are lots of possible ways to go in life, but there really is just ONE WAY, a better way, a way that Jesus leads. Ernest was learning that. Maybe Mr. Dale would learn that too.

Devotion/Study Guide for chapter 4: One Way

Discuss:

Read John 14:1-6

How is Jesus "the way" as he stated in John 14?

What are some of the different ways to go in life as you face choices?

What bothered Ernest about Mr. Dale?

Is there anything in your life that might bother someone around you?

What can you do about that?

Apply:

Choose an area of life in which you can set a goal to go the way of Jesus. Find someone who can keep you accountable in that area of life.

Pray:

Ask God for strength to follow where He leads—especially in the area or areas that are very challenging to you. Thank Him for sending His Son to show you the way.

One Voice

Chapter Five

———————————

"The voice of the LORD echoes above the sea.

The God of glory thunders...

The voice of the LORD is powerful;

the voice of the LORD is full of majesty.

The voice of the LORD splits the mighty cedars...

The voice of the LORD strikes with lightning bolts.

The voice of the LORD makes the desert quake...

The voice of the LORD twists mighty oaks...

In his Temple everyone shouts, "Glory!"

Psalm 29:3-9

H arrison is generally a quiet little place. Especially in the winter things calm down a lot. The "snowbirds" have made their way down to Florida or Arizona—somewhere where the temperatures don't get lower than your shoe size. Budd Lake no longer roars with the sound of boat motors. Instead, eager fishermen wait for the ice to get thick so they can construct their ice fishing shanties. Traffic is lighter at the corner of First and

Main. You hardly need that traffic light in the winter. Downtown, the sound of Christmas music replaces the noise of tourists.

Mr. and Mrs. Thorpe would have loved to experience some of that quietness. With three children in the house—three very active children—there were too many voices to listen to. Everyone was talking at once! Little James, now nearly one and one-half, talked and babbled non-stop. It was his new hobby—that and house dismantling.

"Oh for the days of just eating and sleeping!" Mrs. Thorpe thought.

Karen was into a new verbal experience, too. She was spelling everything. If you asked her a question she would respond: "Y-e-s d-a-d," or "N-o M-o-m." "What would you like to drink, Karen?" "M-i-l-k, d-a-d."

Adding to the conversational mix was Ernest Thorpe. He was into grunting and rolling his eyes. Karen would try to spell "pass the chicken, please," and Ernest would respond with a good grunt and roll of the eyes.

You can imagine the chore it was for Mr. and Mrs. Thorpe to try to have a conversation, let alone hold a thought. Between refereeing arguments, picking up James' food off the floor and trying to get non-spelled answers, Mr. and Mrs. Thorpe couldn't talk to each other. There were just too many voices.

That was also true outside of family conversation. The phone never stopped ringing. Mrs. Thorpe seemed to be a main contact point for school Christmas activity. Everyone had questions, ideas, and more meetings to schedule. Aunt Leona kept

44

calling, too. She was coming over for Christmas dinner this year and kept telling Mrs. Thorpe, "Ham will never do, honey. Ham will never do."

A couple of Mr. Thorpe's co-workers were relentless in their Christmas criticism. They kept saying how lousy this time of year is. "It's a big hassle! Why don't they just abolish Christmas." Mr. Thorpe felt like he was working with the Grinch's brothers.

Even at church tension was running high. Mrs. Schliefmann, the Sunday School Superintendent, was getting very worried about the Christmas program this year. As she tried to teach lines, play piano accompaniments, and lead groups through their stage movements, she was getting exasperated. A few parents heard her vowing to the pastor that she was never getting involved again!

And guess who was fixing the garage door back at the Thorpe homestead—yes, the garage door that Ernest backed into during his driving mishap? Coincidences are amazing around the holidays! Mr. Thorpe called C & D Carpentry Company. They came highly recommended. It turned out that the "D" in "C & D" stood for "Dale." As in Mr. Dale. As in Lisa's Father, the loud, yelling man at Ernest's Behind the Wheel classes at school. The family soon discovered that he did not mellow out in a domestic setting. Mrs. Thorpe had to keep James out of hearing range because Mr. Dale's vocabulary was not fit for children. Mrs. Thorpe tried to be kind and smooth out his bad attitude with a little Christmas encouragement, but it was no use.

"I can't wait 'til this month is over!" Mr. Dale shouted.

Karen said that Mr. Dale was a g-r-u-m-p.

Yes, there were too many voices putting the pressure on and making this one of the most stressful Christmases ever.

On Sunday evening, after a tiring week, Mr. and Mrs. Thorpe sat together on the couch and looked at the Christmas tree. The lights were beautiful. The house was reasonably quiet. On Sunday nights the kids had to p-l-a-y and give mom her quiet time. James was in the room with mom and dad. But he was actually quiet as he played with his mom's slippers. Mr. and Mrs. Thorpe were tired, drained, and sad.

> *There were too many voices putting pressure on and making this one of the most stressful Christmases ever.*

"It just shouldn't be this way," Mrs. Thorpe said quietly. "I feel like giving up."

Mr. Thorpe opened their Bible and looked up the word "encouragement" in the concordance. Romans 15 stood out, so he looked it up. Then he read, *"For everything that was written in the past was written to teach us, so that through endurance and the encouragement of the Scriptures we might have hope. May the God who gives endurance and encouragement give you a spirit of unity among yourselves as you follow Christ Jesus, so that with one heart and mouth you may glorify the God and Father of our Lord Jesus Christ"(vss.4-5).*

The endurance and the encouragement of the Scriptures. God who gives endurance and encouragement. His gracious voice for hope. Sometimes the ONE VOICE you need to hear gets drowned out by all the other voices that are so loud and dominant. Sometimes you need to hear a voice that puts life into you instead of one that takes life out of you. That's the ONE VOICE Mr. and Mrs. Thorpe needed to hear after that long week and through their pre-Christmas days. It was the prevailing and ever-faithful voice of their Lord and Savior through life. Nothing could stop the baby in Bethlehem, the teacher with His disciples, the Christ on the cross carrying our sin, the risen Lord Jesus from death and the grave. His voice of the forgiveness of sins, new life and eternal salvation is the ONE VOICE that brings us back to where we need to be, to where it's best to be.

Mr. Thorpe read some more: *"May the God of hope fill you with all joy and peace as you trust in him, so that you may overflow with hope by the power of the Holy Spirit"(vs.13).* One voice to fill life up again. Mr. and Mrs. Thorpe needed that. And on that December Sunday evening that ONE VOICE was heard.

Just then James said, "Jesus!" He was pointing to the manger scene ornaments on the Christmas tree. Perfect timing. Mr. Thorpe joked, "J-e-s-u-s." Mr. and Mrs. Thorpe laughed. No matter how you said it, it was one welcome voice.

The next day Mrs. Thorpe and James went to the Mall in Mount Pleasant to do some final Christmas shopping. Every time James saw a Christmas tree in a store or in the mall he would shout out: "Jesus!" He was thinking about the ornaments at home. Above the many voices of the shoppers that day, ONE VOICE was being heard. "Jesus!" all through the stores. Mrs. Thorpe did not try to quiet James down.

As the family sat around the table that evening, Ernest had some news to share. He was talking to Lisa Dale at lunch. Ernest found out that five years ago Lisa's mom was very sick with cancer. On December 20th, five years ago, Mrs. Dale died. Mr. and Mrs. Thorpe looked at each other. That's why. Now they understood the man fixing their garage door. Now they knew what he needed.

Oh, how the endurance, the encouragement and the hope of the Lord needed to be heard. You can't always see everyone's heartache. And life can empty you out. But there is ONE VOICE, ONE wonderful VOICE that can fill you back up.

Devotion/Study Guide for chapter 5: One Voice

Discuss:

Hosea 2:14-20

In these verses God describes Himself as a man asking a woman to marry him. This represents God's attitude toward us. How does God's voice contrast with the many voices in your life?

What voices compete for your attention?

What voices affect the way you feel about yourself?

How does God's voice make a difference for the better in your life?

Apply:

List a voice or two that you've been listening to way too much these days.

Now list the qualities of God's voice and message to you from Hosea chapter 2.

Talk about how you can make sure you hear God's voice more than the many voices of the world.

Pray:

Thank God for speaking to you in a loving, caring and edifying way. Thank Him specifically for one way His voice has encouraged you this week.

49

Handling Life's Hardships
One Day
Chapter Six

"In that day they will say, 'Surely this is our God; we trusted in him, and he saved us. This is the LORD, we trusted in him; let us rejoice and be glad in his salvation.'" Isaiah 25:9

I n Harrison not a lot of patience was left the week before Christmas. Beneath the snow-covered roofs of that little town, life was restless and pushing to move ahead. Not much progress was being felt, however. You see, the week before Christmas was a time of family visiting. With all of Mr. Thorpe's brothers and sisters, the visits had to start well before Christmas if everyone was going to get to see each other. And this was the day for the annual Christmas visit to Uncle Ben's house in the country.

Uncle Ben did not make or grow rice. He was a little tired of that joke. He was a farmer, however. And Uncle Ben's house in the country was not really the favorite place to visit. It was a nice place, but kind of old. The house smelled a little bit—that farm smell that Ernest and Karen weren't used to. The television reception was terrible, so they couldn't really watch much. Besides, the dads were all trying to tune in to the football game. The other adults just sat around and talked. Karen couldn't wait to go home, but she found something to do when she located an old Christmas catalogue. Looking at all the toys reminded her how much she couldn't wait to open her Christmas presents.

One of the sisters-in-law, Aunt Allison, was talking about how she couldn't wait to get into their new house. It was big. The kitchen had every kind of new convenience possible. The family was getting a satellite dish, too. This was a "dream house," Aunt Allison said. While she talked, she stood. In fact, the whole time Aunt Allison was at Uncle Ben's house, she stood. She didn't like sitting on the old furniture. You did sink in when you sat down, and the furniture at Uncle Ben's wasn't in the best condition. Aunt Allison only sat down when it was time to eat. There was a metal folding chair for that. Aunt Allison put a napkin on the folding chair before she sat down—just to be on the safe side. After she got comfortable she reminded everyone who might not have heard it before that she couldn't wait for her new place.

Her husband, Uncle Ed, chimed in, "I can't wait for Ben to get cable! I can hardly see the football game!"

Mr. Thorpe added, "I can't wait to eat! I'm starving!"

During dinner, Aunt Amy, Ben's wife, said to Mrs. Thorpe, "I bet you can't wait until James is on his own a little bit more." Mrs. Thorpe just smiled politely. She was actually enjoying this last opportunity to be mom to a little one.

It seemed that everybody in that room was looking ahead to something else.

Ernest Thorpe wasn't interested in the football game on TV, the Christmas catalogue, the talk with the adults, or even the food. When Ernest was at Uncle Ben's, he was interested in Uncle Ben's office. It was a small room. There were two French doors on the outside wall that gave a view of the snowy fields. The room was crowded with a small desk and two little book cases. The walls had bulletin boards on them, and they were packed with papers—all of Uncle Ben's farm stuff. What intrigued Ernest were Uncle Ben's military medals and items of army memorabilia. They were stuck to a bulletin board just above his desk. A "John-Deere" calendar from two years before hid some of the items, but they were visible enough to grab Ernest's interest. These items were not on display. But they were there. There were old photos, patches, and a name patch that said "Thorpe."

They were from Vietnam. Location names were scribbled on some of the pictures. They were names Ernest could hardly pronounce. Uncle Ben didn't talk about his army life much. But that day, as Ernest looked and wondered, Uncle Ben walked into his office.

He startled Ernest. Uncle Ben didn't seem to mind that Ernest was there. Ernest asked, "What was it like Uncle Ben?"

> *"I learned, Ernest," Uncle Ben said, "to be thankful for each ONE DAY. I was glad to wake up and to see what God might do that day."*

Uncle Ben sat down. "It was one day at a time, Ernest, one day at a time." Uncle Ben went on to describe where he was in Vietnam. He talked about the thick, hot and wet jungle. He talked about the traps, the snipers, and the unseen enemy. He talked about the smells and the sounds. He talked about friends who were left behind.

"I learned, Ernest," Uncle Ben said, "to be thankful for each ONE DAY. I was glad to wake up and to see what God might do that day. I couldn't miss out on the one day He was giving me. It was for my safety and for my peace of mind. Everyone leaves battle with something different, Ernest, but I learned about being content, about being patient. It wasn't from my strength. It wasn't even my idea. It was all I had. There was nothing else except that one day in God's hands. And I learned that was a very good thing."

Ernest sat and listened. Uncle Ben picked up a picture that had "Christmas 1968" written on it. It showed a much younger Uncle Ben with his army buddies. They were in a tropical setting, looked pretty ragged, and were holding up an improvised Christmas tree. In the picture Uncle Ben was holding up a sign that said, "Peace on Earth."

"That was a special Christmas," Uncle Ben continued. "One of my buddies had just died. He didn't get shot or anything. He died of a drug overdose. I think he was trying to escape everything that was happening over there. That was on December 23rd. After my buddy died I think I finally realized what Christmas really meant. It finally hit me that there was real help for what we were going through over there. And it all started on one day—the day that God came into our world. That Christmas I realized how important it is to have real help, a real Savior. Jesus suffered more than I did or ever will. And He made it through. He made it through to bring me through. So I made that sign and helped decorate that tree. It was in memory of Alex, my friend. And it was a way of holding on to real help—one day at a time."

Uncle Ben reflected, "I didn't want a career of working at the family farm when I left for Vietnam, but when I came back, I saw something very special happening here."

54

Uncle Ben opened the old looking Bible on his desk. It was next to the day's issue of USA TODAY. He read from James chapter five: *"Be patient, then, brothers, until the Lord's coming. See how the farmer waits for the land to yield its valuable crop and how patient he is for the autumn and spring rains. You too, be patient and stand firm, because the Lord's coming is near" (Vss.7-8).*

"Each ONE DAY around here," Uncle Ben said as he looked out the French doors, "is ONE DAY with the Lord doing His special work. And I know that on the ONE DAY He chooses, He'll be back to put it all together in just the right way, forever. It puts a lot in perspective, Ernest. I try to live my life with that perspective."

After Uncle Ben answered some questions and explained his patches and medals to Ernest, they left that little office and went back out into the hubbub. Everyone was still talking. There were statements like: "I can't wait!" and "It's too slow." Aunt Allison, discussing some construction glitches, said, "It seems like nothing is happening!" Ernest looked at Uncle Ben. There was plenty happening. Right now. It was another ONE DAY with Jesus, the Savior, with us and working hard. Ernest had a new perspective after his Christmas visit at Uncle Ben's.

Devotion/Study Guide for chapter 6: One Day

Discuss:

Read Hebrews 3:1-13

These verses give warnings about straying from God's ways. What is important for each day to keep your walk with God strong?

What important thing did Uncle Ben learn in Vietnam?

What did Ernest realize about each day?

Apply:

What future event or hope have you been dwelling on?

Has that caused you to miss out on the importance of each day that God has given you?

Why is today important for you according to God?

Pray:

Thank God for this day. Thank Him for one way you see Him working in your life and through your life.

Handling Life's Hardships
One Savior
Chapter Seven

———————————

"See, your Savior comes!" Isaiah 62:11

T here are a lot of gaps that open up around Christmas time—and I'm not referring to the clothing store chain. I'm talking about the emptiness you might feel. We're not alone. There were gaps for the folks in Harrison too. Things were missing. Some of the Christmas lights from around town had been swiped by a few wild kids who were out much too late. There were gaps in people's memory as they tried to keep up with everything they had to do. There were gaps in families as some couldn't get together with loved ones who were too far away. There were gaps in energy levels as people were too tired to do everything on their pre-Christmas lists. Even some letters from the Bucilli's Pizza sign were missing. The winter winds did some damage. The sign used to read: "All you can eat buffet - Tuesday." Now, the "U"'s were missing.

At the Thorpe house Jesus was missing! He was gone. It was the Jesus in the manger scene. Karen couldn't leave him alone. Every year she stole him from the manger scene that was set up beneath the Christmas tree. And every year it was getting more difficult to find him. Karen said, "I can't remember where I put him." Mrs. Thorpe was intent on tracking down the most important part of her manger scene. She wanted to find him. A missing Jesus just wouldn't do.

After scouring the house and checking all of Karen's traditional hiding places, Mrs. Thorpe had to take a break. There was too much to be done. She had to make a trip to the IGA to shop for some final food items for Christmas dinner. Some last minute gift shopping had to be done. And then there were the Christmas cards—getting later and later every year. Mr. Thorpe would have to run down to the post office once the cards were finished. Any gaps in time availability were being filled very quickly.

> *Here was a man with questions. Here was a man with sadness, anger and emptiness. Here was a man who needed good hope in his life, some joy and comfort.*

And then there was Mr. Dale, the angry father who yelled at the Driver's Ed. teacher every time Ernest went to his Behind the Wheel classes, the man who fixed the Thorpe's garage door and who couldn't wait until Christmas was over, and the man whose wife died five years ago just before Christmas.

Mrs. Thorpe did not forget about Mr. Dale. Here was a man who was hurting. Here was a man with questions. Here was a man with sadness, anger and emptiness. Here was a man who needed good hope in his life, some joy and comfort. Mr. Dale was on Mrs. Thorpe's heart. She had to reach out to him. So she decided to push the Christmas cards aside, to let the appetizer tray planning for the Christmas gathering wait, and to write a letter. It went like this:

Dear Mr. Dale,

It seems like yesterday, but it was longer ago that my dear mother died. She was too young, and we were best friends. You know how the sadness feels. My words on paper can't describe it well enough. And even now, with tears in my eyes, I write about those days. What happens to you when one you love dies? You're broken deep inside your soul. You realize what is most important in life and what you want to last. There's no fooling you anymore. I was angry and hurt. But that did not fill my emptiness. In my tiring sadness I was turned to One who could mend me. Slowly He is mending still. Without my Savior, my broken life would remain. If slow mending is what you can use, my family would be honored to sit with you and Lisa on Christmas Eve at St. Luke Lutheran Church. It will be a time to hear of the Savior who mends. Please let us know. We'll save seats next to us.

Very truly yours,

Mrs. Thorpe

It seemed that in a blink of an eye Christmas Eve arrived. There was still so much to do and so much to think about. And to top off all the hustle and bustle, Mrs. Thorpe was still looking for the manger scene Jesus. Where could he be? There was only one Jesus who would fit in that manger scene. No other Jesus would do. And Mrs. Thorpe HAD to find him! She left no cushion unturned as she searched and searched with no help from Karen, of course. It was no use. Where could Jesus be?

It was time to go to St. Luke Lutheran for the Christmas Eve worship service. The Thorpe family settled in at church and saved two seats, one for Mr. Dale and one for Lisa. The service began with "O Come, All Ye Faithful." The worshippers stood to sing, and as they got to the line "Oh, come, let us adore Him," Mr. Dale and Lisa squeezed in and took their places in the seats the Thorpe's had saved. Amazing! Mr. Dale smiled a very small and inconspicuous smile as Mrs. Thorpe glanced at him. He nodded as if to say, "Thank you."

Pastor Graff read from Matthew chapter one: *"But after [Joseph] had considered this, an angel of the Lord appeared to him in a dream and said, 'Joseph, son of David, do not be afraid to take Mary home as your wife, because what is conceived in her is from the Holy Spirit. She will give birth to a son, and you are to give him the name Jesus, because he will save his people from their sins.'"* *(vss.20-21)*. Pastor Graff also read from Romans chapter one, *"And you also are among those who are called to belong to Jesus Christ"(vs.6).*

Those words seemed to reach out into the crowd of worshippers, into lives with gaps. Mrs. Thorpe prayed that those words would reach into Mr. Dale's life.

The next song was "O Little Town of Bethlehem." Mrs. Thorpe saw Mr. Dale singing. On the last verse Mrs. Thorpe prayed as she sang:

O holy Child of Bethlehem,

Descend to us we pray;
Cast out our sin, And enter in,
Be born in us today.
We hear the Christmas angels
The great glad tidings tell;
Oh, come to us, Abide with us,
Our Lord Immanuel!

It was the beginning of being on the mend. The ONE SAVIOR who could fill life's gaps was at work.

It was time to sing "Silent Night" and light the candles:

Silent night, holy night!
Son of God, love's pure light
Radiant beams from your holy face
With the dawn of redeeming grace,
Jesus, Lord, at your birth,
Jesus, Lord at your birth.

During this verse Mrs. Thorpe looked down at Karen. What do you think she saw? There was Jesus—the Jesus from the manger scene. Jesus was in Karen's hand, and as Karen sang, she looked intently at the Christ-child and smiled. Jesus was found! He was found! Or was it the other way around, Mrs. Thorpe thought—aren't we really the ones in His hand? Aren't we really the ones who are found?

That Christmas Eve Jesus was in the right place. The ONE SAVIOR needed, and the ONE SAVIOR given.

Devotion/Study Guide for chapter 7: One Savior

Discuss:

Read Luke 2:10-11

Why is the news of a Savior good news in your life?

Do you ever feel like Jesus is missing?

What are some ways He has found you?

How did Mrs. Thorpe's letter give Mr. Dale what he needed?

Do you ever need mending? How does God help you?

Apply:

Think of one person in your life who needs some mending for his or her soul. Think of one way you can help provide that this week.

Pray:

Thank Jesus for being your Savior. Let Him know specific ways He has saved you.

Handling Life's Hardships
One Fed
Chapter Eight

"Then Jesus declared, 'I am the bread of life. He who comes to me will never go hungry, and he who believes in me will never be thirsty.'" John 6:35

I t was a wonderful Christmas Eve worship time for the people gathered at St. Luke Lutheran Church in Harrison. It was so meaningful, so beautiful. For Pastor Graff, however, it was just past mid-point in a grueling holiday schedule. He had five worship services to prepare for that week. That meant five sermons and too many late nights of study and planning. The days were filled with visits to the sick and homebound, meetings with families who were even more troubled during the holidays, and attempts to track down a plumber who could fix the men's restroom before the Christmas services were in full swing. During those days it was even difficult to break away for Christmas shopping.

Pastor Graff felt emptied out. He missed his wife. He missed his home. And he didn't know what he was going to preach about for Christmas Day. The juices weren't flowing. The well had run dry. As he drove to the hospital for an emergency call, he tried to come up with a message theme. He couldn't do it.

"Maybe it's just too much for me," Pastor Graff thought. Maybe I'm not cut out for this job."

After the 11:00 p.m. Christmas Eve Service Pastor Graff went home. He had to preach the next day at 10:00 a.m., and he didn't even have an idea written down. Pastor Graff and his wife sat on the couch in their living room and looked at the Christmas tree. It was past midnight.

"Merry Christmas," they whispered to each other. They gave each other a Christmas kiss.

"Relax," Mrs. Graff said. "Listen to this." Mrs. Graff read from her Bible:

> *"And there were shepherds living out in the fields nearby, keeping watch over their flocks at night. An angel of the Lord appeared to them, and the glory of the Lord shone around them, and they were terrified. But the angel said to them, 'Do not be afraid. I bring you good news of great joy that will be for all the people. Today in the town of David a Savior has been born to you; he is Christ the Lord. This will be a sign to you: You will find a baby wrapped in cloths and lying in a manger.' Suddenly a great company of the heavenly host appeared with the angel, praising God and saying, 'Glory to God in the highest, and on earth peace, good will toward men!' When the angels had left them and gone into heaven, the shepherds said to one another, 'Let's go to Bethlehem and see this thing that has happened, which the Lord has told us about.' So they hurried off and found Mary and Joseph, and the baby, who was lying in the manger" (Luke 2:6-16).*

Pastor and Mrs. Graff headed off to bed.

Pastor Graff thought, "A manger. A manger." Before he went into the bedroom, he stopped at his desk, sat down, opened his Bible and hymnal, and began to write:

Away in a manger, no crib for a bed,
The little Lord Jesus laid down his sweet head.
The stars in the bright sky looked down where he lay.
The little Lord Jesus asleep on the hay.

Away in a manger, it was a trough for food,
Where animals ate from in that stable so crude.
Removed from the public, this lowly birth place
Was what angels proclaimed as the dawn of God's grace!

Away in a manger, Jesus wasn't alone.
Do you feel "away" too—maybe here or at home?
Do you feel apart from the flow—in a daze?
Are you facing some challenges for your life's ways?

It's not just a manger that makes you feel AWAY.
It's stores and visits and a stressful holiday.
It's people shouting "More!", and TWO fruitcakes from Aunt Bess.
It's shopping and returns and a house that's a mess!

And inside your heart, feeling AWAY can be strong.
You miss your dear loved ones, dear ones who are gone.
And a jolly, jingly season can make emptiness grow.
AWAY, you can feel, not full and not whole.

Steps Forward

AWAY is real life, and what can the world give?
What theory or technology can really help you live?
Can lasting hope or direction be found on TV?
We need more than just us. We need light to see.

So away in a manger, the Savior was born;
God came among us that first Christmas morn!
To help us who are helpless, to answer life's dread,
Jesus Christ, God's Son, was laid in that manger bed.

It was a bed not for rest but for feeding His sheep;
It was a trough of nourishment for all who would weep.
And for all caught in sin and confusion and strife
This manger was bed for our Lord, the Bread of Life.

Away in a manger and away on a cross,
Our caring Lord Jesus in life suffered loss.
He emptied Himself to fill you and more;
His death and arising opened heaven's door.

Away in a manger, a place not for rest,
But for serving your life—Jesus gave you His best.
When you're feeling empty, when there's nothing more you can
give,
Jesus seeks and He saves; He lets the lost live.

In the feeding trough there's food, it lasts and is good;
It's Christ's guiding Word, His body and blood.
When you feel AWAY, when life's too big a dose,
The open arms of Jesus and His Spirit bring you close.

Handling Life's Hardships – One Fed

Now it's into the day of this Christmas you go.
Like the shepherds you've seen Jesus; the Savior you know.
It's not just a charming story and rhyme.
This is what impacts your life for all time!

Like the shepherds you can move past the same old, same old.
You are changed, life is new, hope and blessing unfold.
You can make a difference for the people you love;
There's hope from the Savior, from Jesus above.

And no matter what happens, however AWAY you feel,
While life is not easy, Jesus' help is so real.
And when our footsteps on this earth are all through,
The promise of life at peace is for you!

So, be near me, Lord Jesus; I ask thee to stay
Close by me forever and love me, I pray.
Bless all the dear children in thy tender care,
And take us to heaven to live with thee there. Amen.

That's what Pastor Graff preached on Christmas morning.
ONE FED was helping to feed God's flock. The nourishment was
in the manger.

Devotion/Study Guide for chapter 8: One Fed

Discuss:

Read John 6:35

What does Jesus mean in this verse?

Have you ever felt like Pastor Graff did?

What did God provide to help you out?

Are you being fed with anything that is hurting your life or the lives of your loved ones?

How can you get Jesus' "diet" to be a bigger part of your life?

Apply:

Look at Pastor Graff's poem and identify one or two lines that have special meaning for you.

Pray:

Thank God for feeding you with His Word of life today. Tell Him one way you feel "filled up" again.

Handling Life's Hardships
One More Time
Chapter Nine

———————

*"Because of the Lord's great love we are not consumed, for his
compassions never fail. They are new every morning..."*

Lamentations 3:22-23

C hristmas was over in Harrison, Michigan. Mr. and Mrs.
Thorpe read in the paper that the phone companies
experienced a 17% decline in calls the day after Christmas.
Chicago saw a 10% decline of passengers on their commuter rail
line. And in New York, the stock exchange had its lowest volume
since July third. Even the New York City power lunch spots were
slower than ever.

It was a slow week all over the country. It was anything
BUT slow for the Thorpe family. Three children, all home from
school for two straight weeks, doesn't add up to slow. The day
after Christmas meant tired children, fighting children, loud and
active children. For the first time in her life Mrs. Thorpe wished
that her home could be more like New York City—slower. Just a
little slower.

The three Thorpe children, years apart in age, seemed like
triplets! James, almost a year and a half, did his own thing, didn't
listen, and was constantly getting into where he didn't belong.

Karen, almost seven and a half, did her own thing, didn't listen, and was constantly reminding mom and dad that she wasn't going to listen! Whether it was a request to get dressed, eat her supper, or answer when someone was speaking to her, Karen's reply would be, "No, I don't have to." If her parents told her that it was cold outside, or that the sun was shining, or that the sky was blue, Karen would respond, "No it's not!" She knew everything and her parents knew nothing. Her parents even tried to slow down her stubborn will by making her stand in the corner. It wasn't working.

And Ernest, the sophomore in high school, also did his own thing, didn't listen, and seemed to start more fights over that Christmas vacation than he ever did when he was younger.

Mr. and Mrs. Thorpe had three of the same children! They were just in three different sizes—small, medium and large! Life was not slowing down.

Unfortunately, it just seemed to get worse. Karen received a wonderful book from one of her aunts as a Christmas gift. As she looked through the book, however, she discovered that eight center pages were missing. This was not good. Karen was very attached to this Christmas present. How could something be wrong with it? As Karen got upset, Mrs. Thorpe tried to console her. The book was purchased at the Ben Franklin. All they had to do was to go exchange it.

Mrs. Thorpe and Karen got their coats on, jumped in the car and headed down to the Ben Franklin. Mrs. Thorpe explained the predicament and asked the manager for an exchange. There was a fill-in manager on duty. Apparently Mr. Dobbs, the regular manager who knew the Thorpe family, was on vacation. The fill-in manager asked for a receipt. Mrs. Thorpe explained that her sister-in-law bought the book and she didn't give the receipt with it. The fill-in manager said, "No receipt, no exchange." And he handed the book back to Mrs. Thorpe.

Mrs. Thorpe pleaded in motherly desperation, "We need a book with all the pages. This was a Christmas gift. Do not sabotage this Christmas vacation any further!" She was getting a little upset.

"No receipt, no exchange," the fill-in manager said coldly. Karen started to cry. They left the store. Life was not slowing down.

Back at home Mr. Thorpe heard about the Ben Franklin encounter. "Wasn't Mr. Dobbs there?" he asked.

He called the fill-in manager. "What was his name?" Mr. Thorpe asked his wife.

"I think it was SCROOGE," she replied.

Mr. Thorpe talked to the manager. "No receipt, no exchange" was the consistent reply.

Ernest, with his friend Andy Oreby, happened to be listening to this heated conversation. The family retreated to the kitchen to regroup and get some lunch. Karen's wails could be heard clearly as Ernest and Andy sat in the living room looking at new Christmas gifts. Ernest looked at Andy. He looked at Karen's Christmas book. It was placed on one of the living room chairs.

Ernest said, "Andy, I need your help with OPERATION EXCHANGE. We're going to get a new book for my sister."

Andy smiled and said, "Let's do it!"

The plan was simple. Enter the Ben Franklin. Andy would be a diversion. At the front of the store where the magazines were displayed, he would ask the manager about an obscure comic book title. While the manager searched, Ernest— with the defective book hidden in his backpack—would quietly exchange the grief causing book with a new and complete model. They would then exit the store with the mission accomplished. Happiness would be restored at home.

The plan went smoothly until the manager, who, though grumpy, was quite industrious, said to Andy, "Let me check in the back for that title." Andy tried to persuade him not to go to all that trouble, but the manager turned down the book aisle just as Ernest was tucking Karen's book replacement into his backpack. Life was not slowing down. The industrious and grumpy fill-in manager did what any law abiding store manager is supposed to do. He called the police. This did not make Mr. and Mrs. Thorpe's day.

Mr. and Mrs. Thorpe couldn't take it anymore. They unwound the complicated mess with the police and the store manager. Mrs. Thorpe's sister-in-law brought the receipt for the book to the store, and they got a new one for Karen. But mom and dad ended up in Pastor Graff's office. They needed to talk to someone about teen troubles and parent pressure.

Mr. And Mrs. Thorpe poured out their souls to Pastor Graff. They talked about the frustration, the constant effort, the ongoing battles, the bad attitudes, the lapses in judgment, and now the police! Both of them were at their limits.

Pastor Graff listened. When the Thorpe's finished venting, Pastor Graff said, "You're not alone. This time of year is a tough time for people. And this time of life is difficult too. Maybe it's not the teenage years or the in between years or the toddler years that are the problem. It could be that you're just tired. You've been saying the same things for fifteen years. Over and over again, day after day, you're reinforcing all the lessons that you want to teach as parents. But the response you expect is not there. It's always one more time. That's the long haul of parenthood. And it's tremendously tiring."

After some more talk, some book recommendations for the Thorpe's, and some prayer, the slightly refreshed parents thanked Pastor Graff for listening and went back home with a little better outlook. The next Sunday evening,

> *"You're not alone. This time of year is a tough time for people. And this time of life is difficult, too."*

New Year's Eve, Grandma came over to watch the kids and Mr. and Mrs. Thorpe went out by themselves. First they would attend the New Year's Eve service at St. Luke Lutheran church. Following the service they had a reservation for dinner at Monte's. Mrs. Thorpe looked forward to her favorite mostaccioli.

At church Pastor Graff talked about the New Year. He read from Isaiah 63, *"I will tell of the kindnesses of the Lord...He said, 'Surely they are my people...' and so he became their Savior. In all their distress he too was distressed, and the angel of his*

73

presence saved them. In his love and mercy he redeemed them; he lifted them up and carried them all the days of old" (vss.7-9).

"Isn't it great," Pastor Graff commented, "that when difficulties and challenges keep coming in life, our faithful Lord keeps bringing His help ONE MORE TIME. His compassion—one more time. His forgiveness and new beginnings—one more time. His love in Jesus—one more time. Lifting you up and carrying you as you are distressed—one more time. That's your faithful Savior. That's your untiring God for you. Tonight, through His Word of life and through His presence in Communion He steps into your life—one more time." Pastor Graff closed out his message by saying that to be redeemed meant that you were part of the best Christmas purchase of all. You have been bought by the Lord, and He will not return you. Nothing will separate you from His love.

After church the Thorpe's enjoyed a wonderful dinner at Monte's. In just a few hours it would be a brand new year. There was more of life to tackle, more parenting to do, more work to accomplish. They would be in the position of giving all their energy ONE MORE TIME.

But that's not all there was in life. The Thorpe's knew that life was not slowing down, but neither was the One who "lifted them up and carried them," the One who redeemed them. Was Christmas really over in Harrison? One thing was certain, because of the untiring love and presence of Jesus, the buying was at an all time high for any life that might hit an all time low.

Devotion/Study Guide for chapter 9: One More Time

Discuss:

Read Jeremiah 7:13

God is frustrated with His stubborn people in these verses, but what does His action show about His attitude toward us?

How did the discovery of this trait of God help Mr. and Mrs. Thorpe?

How does it help you?

How are you in the position of serving or reaching out to someone again and again?

What strength do you need from God to keep it up?

Apply:

Talk about one area of life in which you are tired of the same old grind. Should you or shouldn't you keep it up? How can you get re-energized for this calling from God in your life?

Pray:

Thank God for His persistence in your life—specifically thank Him for one way He has kept up His work for you. Ask Him to give you strength to serve Him for the long haul.

Through the Ordinary
Chapter Ten

"The kingdom of heaven is like treasure hidden in a field."
Matthew 13:44

Y ou could have stopped and looked at the new blades of grass and the flowers beginning to pop up through the wet brown floor of the woods surrounding Harrison. That would have been enough. You could have breathed in that smell of springtime and squished through the ground that was still wet from the melting snow. It would have been enough to refresh you on your walk through Harrison. But there was more. There was more than just the ordinary transition from winter to spring.

A visitor was in town. He was a student from the University who had researched the history of mid-Michigan, and now he was making his detail-filled presentation at a Harrison High School special assembly.

"Who got this guy?" Ernest Thorpe wondered. He was boring. He was like the rest of the special speakers the students were rounded up to listen to.

"It was probably Mr. Blob," Paul Tucker whispered to Ernest. That was the history teacher—at least he was known to the students by that name. History was not the most popular subject at Harrison High. And Ernest and Paul were not interested in this assembly speaker at all—until they heard the word "TREASURE." Treasure!

"Back during the depression, in 1930," the assembly speaker said, "a bag of money was lost in a rail shipment from Detroit to Traverse City. Rumor had it that it was lost somewhere around Harrison. It wasn't discovered to be missing until much later. But the money was never found. Some old-timers said that a map to the treasure was made. And the treasure might still exist right around here."

Chills went through Ernest and Paul. They looked at each other with eyes wide open. All they could talk about on the way home from school was TREASURE. Harrison was a lot more exciting with the possibility of something hidden and valuable waiting to be found.

As the days went by the talk and dreams about treasure faded. School work had to be done. Track practice had started. The assembly and the excitement were in the past. One Saturday, about a month after Ernest and Paul had heard about the treasure, the two friends were hiking in a field behind the old Critman place. Mr. Critman had died a long time ago. A nephew had been taking care of the property until he died too. Now it was abandoned. The little wooden house was run down. There was an old barn not too far from the house, and a silo next to the barn. The silo was made of stone. County workers had knocked out part of the silo wall at the bottom so no one would get trapped inside. Ernest and Paul decided to take a look.

The silo was empty. There wasn't much exciting about it. But as Paul scanned the ground, he saw a jagged piece of stone sticking up against the wall. Paul pulled on it and it moved. Ernest knelt down to help. They dug and pulled. What was this stone? It was flat and had a greenish color. Finally they pulled it out of the ground. It was about the size of a notebook. Paul cleaned the mud off with his sleeve. Letters and other marks were carved into one side of what looked like a piece of slate.

Paul said, "Ernest! Take a look at this! It looks like a map!"

Sure enough. It was a map. At the top was carved "B. Critman 1930." There were squares and lines and even an "X" on the map. One word came into the minds of Ernest and Paul: TREASURE! They got chills again as they looked at the map. Their hearts pounded. There was more to life in Harrison than met the eye!

Ernest and Paul carried the slate map back to Paul's house. His mom and dad were working and his sister was gone, so they could clean the map off and take a good look at it in private. They rubbed two patterns of the map on paper—one for Ernest and one for Paul. Paul put the piece of slate under his bed.

"No one's going to find it here," he said.

Ernest didn't argue. It didn't even smell good under there.

Then they planned. Throughout the week they went to the library to check out the old county survey maps. If they could figure out what the markings meant, what those squares and lines represented, it could mean TREASURE!

All week after school Ernest and Paul searched for information. They thought they knew Harrison—every nook and cranny. Was there something they didn't know? Was there something still to be discovered? Could there be a surprise in it for them?

After painstaking work looking through old and dusty records, they finally found a map that had the Critman property on it. In addition to the old buildings Ernest and Paul had seen, it looked like there were two large sheds that once stood north of the house. They also saw that the railroad tracks ran through the northwest part of the property. The two squares on the map must have been those two sheds. If they went due north halfway to the creek, then west from there, they should find an old well. That was where the "X" was on the map!

> *Was there something they didn't know? Was there something still to be discovered? Could there be a surprise in it for them?*

Early the next Saturday Ernest and Paul went back to the Critman place. From the house they walked carefully to try to find evidence of the two sheds. It didn't take long to locate the old foundations. It was just a matter of knowing what to look for. The two treasure hunters paced off the distance to the creek and walked half-way back. They turned west with paper maps in hand, and they walked straight ahead, looking at the ground with each step. Finally, they hit a small open spot in the otherwise overgrown grassy area. There appeared to be a piece of cement peeking out of the ground! Ernest and Paul dug with their hands. They uncovered a square of roughly poured cement. This must be the place! It just might be true! All this time! Right under their noses! The prospect of treasure had their hearts pounding again. But even though they tried with all their might, they couldn't budge the cement square.

"We need help," Ernest said. "I'll get my dad."

Ernest went home and explained the whole thing to his dad—the assembly, the discovery, the treasure.

"Here's the map," Ernest said.

Mr. Thorpe went with him to take a look. Sure enough. There was something to this. Even with Mr. Thorpe's help, however, that cement square was staying put. Mr. Thorpe knew what they needed to do. Ernest and Paul got in the truck and Mr. Thorpe drove them to the county office building in town. Mr. Thorpe asked Red Michaels, his friend who worked at the county office, about the land. Red checked his files. He reported to Mr. Thorpe that there was no owner of the land and it would probably just go up for auction. Mr. Thorpe explained the situation. Red told him, with a chuckle, that he could feel free to look for treasure.

Mr. Thorpe gave Ernest and Paul the thumbs up, stopped at the house to get some cable and hooks, and headed back to the Critman property. They were going to move that slab with the help of four-wheel drive! They hooked the cables up, but even though the slab was moving, Mr. Thorpe couldn't get the traction he needed.

"We need some more horsepower," he told the boys.

What about Pastor Graff? He lived just up the road and had his own four-wheel-drive truck. It was a go! The group hurried to Pastor Graff's house. They explained the whole adventure to him. Pastor Graff was intrigued.

"Treasure, eh?" Pastor Graff stroked his chin in thought. "Let's go get it!"

Now there were two trucks pulling on the cement square. After a rev of the engines, the trucks were put into gear. Slowly, but with ease, the cement square gave way.

Ernest and Paul were the first ones to look. There was a round opening. Inside was a metal box. It was rusted. The lock was broken. Four sets of eyes stared as Ernest and Paul opened the box with trembling hands. Inside there was an old Bible. Papers were tucked into it. One of the papers was a written newspaper announcement that a satchel was found. The article gave a brief description of the satchel and described the location where it was discovered. The newspaper note asked anyone who recognized the lost item to meet with the finder, identify it, and claim it. The name at the bottom of the announcement was B. Critman.

Another paper tucked into the Bible was from the county. It was a written record of the satchel found and the amount of money in it—$10,000. At the bottom of the note was a word stamped in red ink: "Unclaimed."

Finally there was a pad of paper. It appeared to be a list. There were dates in the first column. The first date written was six months after the newspaper announcement. The second column on this pad listed names of families and an amount of money next to each of the names. In a third column were words like "food," "doctor," "medicine," and "supplies."

Mr. Thorpe scanned the pad of paper and flipped through the many pages. He said, "It looks like B. Critman found the money, tried to return it, and then gave it to families who were in bad shape during the depression."

Everyone was silent, trying to grasp what they had just found.

Ernest was holding the Bible. He noticed that some of the verses were circled on the pages in which the papers were tucked.

Ernest said, "Listen to this. Here are the verses that B. Critman must have circled: *"For you know that it was not with perishable things such as silver or gold that you were redeemed from the empty way of life handed down to you from your forefathers, but with the precious blood of Christ, a lamb without blemish or defect. He was chosen before the creation of the world, but was revealed in these last times for your sake. Through him you believe in God, who raised him from the dead and glorified him, and so your faith and hope are in God. Now that you have purified yourselves by obeying the truth so that you have sincere love for your brothers, love one another deeply, from the heart"* (1 Peter 1:18-22).

Everybody listened and wondered about what they just found and heard.

Finally Pastor Graff spoke quietly, "This is a treasure!"

What a turn of events in Harrison! Through the ordinary days and routine happenings, adventure had unfolded. Of course it made the newspaper. Right on the front page there was a picture of Ernest and Paul standing next to the metal strongbox. Each of them had a hand on the slate map they found.

That evening Pastor Graff worked on his sermon. He was reading about Jesus' walk with two men on the road to Emmaus. It was after Jesus' resurrection. Verses 30-32 of Luke 24 said, *"When [Jesus] was at the table with them, he took bread, gave thanks, broke it and began to give it to them. Then their eyes were opened and they recognized him, and he disappeared from their sight. They asked each other, 'Were not our hearts burning within us while he talked with us on the road and opened the Scriptures to us?'"* Their hearts were burning within them. Through the ordinary days and routine happenings, adventure had unfolded. God clued them in to the treasure of forgiveness and new life that was right under their noses.

Sometimes you just don't realize how close real treasure is. As Pastor Graff worked on his sermon, he thought about the treasure-finding adventure of Ernest and Paul. He thought about the treasure-finding adventure of the men on the road to Emmaus, too. And he knew that there was more treasure to be found. That's how God works—through the ordinary.

Devotion/Study Guide for chapter 10: Through the Ordinary

Discuss:

Read Isaiah 33:5-6

What treasure has God given you in your life?

How do you overlook it at times?

What people in your life bring God's treasure to you?

Ernest and Paul got excited about finding treasure. How can you get excited about the treasure God puts in your life?

Apply:

Thank a person in your life for bringing God's treasure to you. Make a list of treasures you never want to forget.

Pray:

Thank God for making your ordinary life a life filled with the treasure of His love and grace. Let Him know one way you see His treasure in your life.

Finding Treasure
In a Blur
Chapter Eleven

"Teach me what I cannot see." Job 34:32

P astor Graff felt like his life was in a blur. It was his turn to host some pastors from the area for a time of worship and discussion. This was a monthly event with several of the Lutheran Churches taking turns. In the summer even more pastors attended—retired men who were spending the warm months up north. Pastor Graff could manage the arrangements that had to be made for the group. He felt comfortable with the sermon he had ready. He was looking forward to some time with his fellow workers in the ministry. Usually it was a mutually refreshing and encouraging time. Pastor Graff was going to try his best to make the day meaningful for his colleagues.

And it was. The day went well—at least that's what Pastor Graff thought. The light breakfast was delicious. The worship and prayer time together was a nice change of pace for men who were used to leading worship services. They got to sit, listen, and receive ministry instead of give it. There was also plenty of conversation and laughter as the pastors visited together.

When it was time to say goodbye, one of the retired gentlemen whom Pastor Graff really didn't know said to him, "You know, you should have worn your robe. You were inappropriately attired to lead worship. It was very disappointing. I am shocked at what this church is coming to."

As he walked out the door the pastor added under his breath, "These young upstarts."

His robe? That's all he noticed? With all the preparation and set-up Pastor Graff didn't have time to put his white clergy robe on. Besides, he felt that a more casual environment might allow for some quality time together—bearing one another's burdens, being one as they worshipped the Lord together. Apparently it didn't turn out that way. His robe. That comment took the wind out of Pastor Graff's sails. Was he wrong? Did he fail? Pastor Graff felt like he was living in a blur.

That afternoon the blur continued. A child in the congregation—a little girl—had a bad fall and hit her head. She was in the hospital and was not doing well. After receiving the phone call Pastor Graff rushed to the hospital. Throughout the day and into the night her condition worsened. And then she was gone. So suddenly, so tragically, this beautiful little girl died. Her family was crushed. Pastor Graff was shaken. Just a few years ago he baptized this little one, and now...what a blur life seemed to be.

How could Pastor Graff carry on with business as usual? He was tired. He was sad. He was drained and discouraged. But the pressure was on to complete all the tasks that had to be done. There were many demands. He had fifteen phone messages to return. Confirmation class lessons needed to be prepared. Preparation for Sunday Bible class was waiting. He had some letters to write and an elders meeting to get ready for.

"O Lord," Pastor Graff prayed, "Help me! I need some major intervention. I need to hear you loudly and clearly." If there was any time for God to send that proverbial lightning bolt from heaven, this would have been it.

But there was no time for him to moan and groan. Pastor Graff was scheduled for a visit to the nursing home in Clare to see Mrs. Marsh, a long time member of St. Luke in Harrison, so off he went.

The nursing home was pleasant. A few residents were gathered in the day room watching a "McCloud" episode on the console color TV. Pastor Graff walked the familiar hallways to Mrs. Marsh's room. He sat in the big chair by the window like he did every month. The chair was next to Mrs. Marsh's bed and close to her wheelchair. She was always in either one of those two spots when Pastor Graff visited. Today Mrs. Marsh was in her wheelchair. This woman of many years wasn't very talkative. She had made it clear to Pastor Graff that she was tired and worn out. Arthritic pain was a constant part of her life. She preferred to be quiet, keep to herself, and wait for the Lord to take her home. Pastor Graff greeted Mrs. Marsh and talked to her. He mentioned some current events and some church news. He read some Psalms to her and he prayed with her.

While he was praying, however, disaster struck. Pastor Graff felt himself falling asleep! The room was very warm. He was tired. He couldn't help it. His eyes were heavy. His head was bobbing. His own voice seemed to be fading into the distance.

Mrs. March squeezed Pastor Graff's hand. "What's wrong, Pastor?" she asked.

Pastor Graff was startled. He couldn't believe that he was falling asleep while he was visiting someone! No one ever told him about this danger during his preparation for the ministry! How was Mrs. Marsh going to feel? Pastor Graff apologized. He was so sorry. He explained to Mrs. Marsh what he had been through. It had been a draining week. He had lots of questions. And he was very tired.

"Mrs. Marsh," Pastor Graff asked, "You've been through a lot in life. What advice would you give to a younger person like me for days like these?"

Pastor Graff didn't expect Mrs. Marsh to say much. Her memory was not very good anymore. She usually answered "I don't know" to Pastor Graff's attempts at conversation. But today was different. Mrs. Marsh lifted her head, looked straight into Pastor Graff's eyes and said, "Stay as you are." Then she put her head back down as she sat in her wheel chair.

Stay as you are. Pastor Graff thanked Mrs. Marsh for the visit and her understanding, and he made his way back home. Her words echoed in his mind. Stay as you are. After he got home Pastor Graff opened his Bible and read:

> *"And the word of the Lord came to him: 'What are you doing here, Elijah?' He replied, 'I have been very zealous for the Lord God Almighty. The Israelites have rejected your covenant, broken down your altars, and put your prophets to death with the sword. I am the only one left, and now they are trying to kill me too.' The Lord said, 'Go out and stand on the mountain in the presence of the Lord, for the Lord is about to pass by.' Then a great and*

powerful wind tore the mountains apart and shattered the rocks before the Lord, but the Lord was not in the wind. After the wind there was an earthquake, but the Lord was not in the earthquake. After the earthquake came a fire, but the Lord was not in the fire. After that came a gentle whisper. When Elijah heard it, he pulled his cloak over his face and went out and stood at the mouth of the cave"(1 Kings 19:9b-13).

Not in the wind, not in the earthquake, not in the fire. It was in the whisper that God spoke to His servant, Elijah. Here was the consistent, steady, and ever-present help for one whose life was in a blur. There was hope for Elijah. God was still in control. He was still leading. And He made that known in the whisper.

Pastor Graff knew that he was tossed, shaken and tired. He also knew that God had sent a gentle whisper into his life. It was a still, small voice that said, "Stay as you are."

What did the words mean? Pastor Graff thought of the Bible verse: *"Jesus Christ is the same yesterday and today and forever"(Hebrews 13:8).* "Stay as you are" meant staying on the course of the One who didn't change, the One who always prevailed, the One who brings life, the One who leads through all the winds, earthquakes and fires of life. Whether it was petty comments about robes or the crushing news about a precious little girl, Jesus Christ is faithful through the journey. There was nothing else anyone could depend on except His help and strength and leadership.

For life in a blur Pastor Graff was glad to hear such a whisper. Do you hear it?

Devotion/Study Guide for chapter 11: In a Blur

Discuss:

Read Psalm 116:1-9

When does life feel like it's a blur to you?

What times of the year take their toll on you?

How does what Pastor Graff discovered through Mrs. Marsh help you when you feel like life is in a blur?

Apply:

Identify God's whisper to you when you were experiencing a difficult time in life. Try to spot the whispers He is providing today.

Pray:

Let God know how life is draining you lately. Ask Him for help. Make a commitment to listen for the help He will give.

Finding Treasure
For a Miracle
Chapter Twelve

———————

"Lord, to whom shall we go? You have the words of eternal life."
John 6:68

H er name was Ruth. The child from St. Luke Lutheran who died. She was just six years old. She decided to have one last run down a hill in her back yard before her family went to the fair. It was a beautiful day—warm and sunny. Ruth was excited about fair rides and homemade fudge. As she took that last run, she tripped and fell head first. Her parents saw it happen. They were waiting by the car calling her to come. As soon as she fell they ran to her. When she didn't move they ran faster calling her name. When they got to her they saw the rock that her head hit and they saw the injury. Ruth's mom ran to the house and dialed 911. Ruth's dad tried to stop the bleeding.

Six-year-old Ruth was rushed to the hospital. Family and friends were called. So was Pastor Graff. Word spread for prayers to be said. The injury was serious. The doctors said that the tests didn't look good. A neurologist was flying up from Detroit. He was one of the best, but the trauma left little Ruth in a coma and fighting for her life.

This kind of tragedy did not happen in Harrison very often. Maybe it didn't seem to happen anywhere that often, or maybe it was just something no one could ever get used to. Word spread quickly through the community. Prayers were lifted up for healing. Prayers for a miracle were said. The people from church and from all over Harrison volunteered to bring meals, to baby-sit for Ruth's little sister, and to do whatever could be done. But in too short a time Ruth died. Just six years old.

Pastor Graff was able to spend a lot of time with Ruth's family through all of this. He waited with them. He prayed with them. He cried with them. Then, the mom and dad who were on their way to the fair had to make their way to the funeral home to plan a funeral for their little girl.

There was no talk about getting over this terrible loss. That would not happen. The family did not want to get over little Ruth. They just needed to get through all of this—through sadness, through tears, through questions, through emptiness, through guilt, through anger, through all of it. They prayed for a miracle of peace and strength.

Hundreds of families gathered at the funeral home to share in the grief of Ruth's family. There had never been a crowd like that at the funeral home before. The day was long and filled with tears. When evening came, Ruth's parents went home and sat in their daughter's room. Her stuffed animals were still just where she put them. She had clothes in a pile that needed to be washed. Her Minnie Mouse bank was open and coins were scattered on the floor. On the day she was going to the fair, Ruth dug four quarters out of her bank to spend there. Above her bed was her favorite picture of Jesus. He was with children. One little girl, as Ruth always pointed out, looked just like her.

Ruth's parents thought about the songs they sang to her as she lay in the hospital—her favorite Jesus songs that she loved to sing and listen to. Ruth's father and mother held each other and cried.

As they tried to talk through the tears, they decided to write something that could be read by Pastor Graff at Ruth's funeral. They took a little pad of paper that was sandwiched in between coloring books in Ruth's closet, a pencil that had printed on it: "Jesus loves me"—Ruth got it from her Sunday School teacher—and they began to write:

> "We prayed for a miracle. Everyone prayed for a miracle. And instead of choosing the miracle of healing, God chose the miracle of eternal life. We know our prayers were answered. We hope and pray that you will not only grieve with us, but that you will give thanks with us for Ruth's new life in heaven. Now we wait with growing love in our hearts to see her again. We do not count the days after her death; we count the days to join her in new life. Thank you for your prayers, for your support, and for all your help through this difficult time. God has shown us another precious miracle through you."

Pastor Graff read those words at Ruth's funeral. The service overflowed with people. The church, the fellowship area, the parking lot and the lawn were filled. Outside speakers were set up for the crowds. It was truly a miracle that so many throughout Harrison were drawn to the Lord of Life through that time of grief and death. It was like the picture of Jesus in Ruth's room—Jesus embracing His children. Every person got a chance to hear about the Lord's miracle of life that day.

Pastor Graff read from Isaiah 56, *"These I will bring to my holy mountain and give them joy in my house of prayer"(vs.7).* The open arms of Jesus were for Ruth and for everyone gathered there. Because of the death and resurrection of Jesus, death was not the end. Now there were footsteps of life—new, forgiven, and restored life. The day would come when the Lord would gather us for a reunion as we walk with Him. Through these days of hurt and sadness it would be step by step, united in prayer, walking with Him, as Ruth does now.

> *They could become bitter and angry. They could lose all hope and give up on life. Or they could keep going.*

These days were hard. And many more hard days were ahead. Ruth's parents knew that only as they were brought close to their Savior would they be able to walk through each day, each minute. This was not a temporary salve or some imaginary help for real and devastating hurt in life. Ruth's parents were faced with many choices as they struggled over their daughter's death. They could become bitter and angry. They could lose all hope and give up on life. Or they could keep going. True, there were moments that all those emotions took hold for a little while. But the question Ruth's parents faced was: what emotion, what course in life, would prevail? As the days of grief unfolded, they experienced the very real response of God to their cries for help. They experienced the miracle of a very real God who cares. And that is what they wanted to have prevail in their lives. They were going to keep loving their Ruth, and they were going to keep trusting their Savior. They knew that, one day, they would all be together again.

Waiting would be very hard—words can't describe it. They knew, however, that it wouldn't be possible to make it were it not for a miracle. And that is exactly what God is best at.

Devotion/Study Guide for chapter 12: For a Miracle

Discuss:

Read Mark 5:32-45

The little girl in the Bible reading was raised back to life, but Ruth wasn't. What miracles did God accomplish for Ruth and her parents?

What miracles have you prayed for that weren't given to you?

What miracles have you seen accomplished in your life?

Apply:

Talk about why God is trustworthy even though you may not receive everything you ask for. Discuss what you think heaven will be like. Why is it the ultimate answer to what we're going through in life now?

Pray:

Thank God for a miracle that you have seen Him do in your life or in the life of a loved one. Ask God for a miracle you need today.

Finding Treasure
On the Job
Chapter Thirteen

"I lift up my eyes to the hills-- where does my help come from? My help comes from the LORD, the Maker of heaven and earth. He will not let your foot slip-- he who watches over you will not slumber." Psalm 121:1-3

S unrise. In Harrison it was always beautiful. On summer days it was especially beautiful! The light of the sun caused the mist that covered Budd Lake to glow as it slowly evaporated. The sunlight pierced the woods and lit up the green leaves like neon lights. Sunrise. It was a favorite time of the day for Mr. Thorpe. Through all the events happening during the summer, the sunrise showed that another new beginning had arrived.

God showed wonderful timing for the Thorpe family that summer. He blessed them with a family flow of events that even kept James happy as he now entered the "terrible two's." The weather had been great. Mrs. Thorpe's garden was growing well. The Thorpe children had healthy looking tans from plenty of outdoor activity. There was plenty of swimming in Budd Lake— the water temperature was up to eighty degrees almost every day. Fishing was good. The bass and muskie were active and biting. Even the Fourth of July fireworks display turned out to be a great family outing. The Thorpe's found a spot across the street from the fairgrounds right at the edge of Wilson State Park. It was a perfect location for watching the summer sky light up with a fantastic array of colors.

Outings to the fair capped off summer activity. Even Karen was enjoying the rides now. Mr. and Mrs. Thorpe were able to take in a Vince Gill concert while Ernest baby-sat his younger sister and brother—a volunteer treat from Ernest to mom and dad during fair week. And, of course, clear summer nights were perfect for a stop at the Dairy Queen or Marvel Freeze. You could sit at an outdoor picnic table and gaze at the stars in the uncluttered Harrison sky.

All seemed well. On this clear summer morning Mr. Thorpe would be putting up a brand new shed that he bought at the Harrison Do-It Center and Lumber Yard. The shed would allow more room for the kids' bikes and outdoor toys. The lawn mower would have a new home in the shed, too. It was getting tiresome moving the car out of the garage every time the grass needed to be cut. God's blessing was clear.

Mr. Thorpe didn't give it a second thought when he was called into the office at the factory on Monday morning. He had a lot of responsibility there and he was consulted frequently about production decisions and personnel matters. What happened, however, was not what Mr. Thorpe expected. The owner of the factory was there along with the shift supervisor. They didn't beat around the bush. The factory was closing, they told Mr. Thorpe. The next two weeks would be a phase-out and shut-down time. After two weeks Mr. Thorpe would no longer have a job. They were sorry, but the business couldn't make it anymore. Mr. Thorpe left the office. He thought of his wife and children. This was not in the plan. He had been working there for fifteen years. He was happy with his job. He was able to provide for his family. And he was planning on making a college education possible for his kids. Ernest was due to start in two years. Now what would happen?

Mr. Thorpe called home right away. He broke the news as gently as he could and reassured his wife. "Everything will be okay," he said, "We'll talk more when I get home."

The summer evening was beautiful. Hot dogs and burgers on the grill was the plan for supper. But everything looked a little different to Mr. Thorpe. After supper he and his wife talked.

"We'll have to work on a financial plan. I'll check unemployment details," Mr. Thorpe said.

"And you'll need to work on a resume," Mrs. Thorpe added. "I can check at the library for some information," she volunteered.

Mr. Thorpe looked at James. He was walking around and singing a song. His little bare feet were ready for a good bath along with the rest of him after a full day of outdoor summer play. Mr. Thorpe looked at his little son and thought about what might happen in life. With no job, how would life be different?

Some might call Mr. Thorpe one dimensional, maybe even simple or naive. His life was not that exciting or sophisticated. It was not a life of high finance or corporate intrigue. There were no TV car chases or mysterious women in his day to day routine— although Karen did get a little mysterious, but she was only eight years old. Mr. Thorpe was simply fighting the good fight of faith each day. He was being faithful through the routine of life. He loved his wife. He loved his children. And He loved his Lord and Savior. Being faithful—that's what real life was all about for him and for the people he knew. And now he had a real-life question to deal with. What was he supposed to do? How would he support his family? That evening he knelt in prayer and asked for the Lord's guidance, strength, and help. Mr. Thorpe was comforted by words of confidence as he read his Bible: *"Oh, the depth of the riches of the wisdom and knowledge of God! How unsearchable his judgments, and his paths beyond tracing out! Who has known the mind of the Lord? Or who has been his counselor? Who has ever given to God, that God should repay him? For from him and through him and to him are all things. To him be the glory forever! Amen"(Romans 11:33-36).* Mr. Thorpe was now on the pathway of trusting God's timing. He really always was, but this was a test of that trust.

Two weeks passed quickly. Mr. and Mrs. Thorpe asked for prayers from friends and church members. They developed a financial plan. They even got a good start on a resume. Mr. Thorpe would have to get a job quickly, however. Unemployment checks would help, but the college fund would have to be used very soon if a job didn't surface. The whole family pitched in to cut expenses—meals at restaurants, luxury items from the grocery store, magazine subscriptions and extra trips with the car. Mr. Thorpe wished he could return that new shed.

Two more weeks went by without even a small lead. Resumes were being sent out. Mr. Thorpe was making phone calls and trying to get interviews, but not much was out there.

Mr. Thorpe thought of adding a new element to his weekly strategy. He called Pastor Graff and asked if they would be able to get together each Monday morning for a brief time of prayer and Bible reading. Monday morning was not a good contact time at companies, so why not make some spiritual contact? Why not get some strength and direction from the Lord? Pastor Graff agreed and suggested that other unemployed folks be invited.

"Why not get the week started right for other people too?" he said.

> *Even when we are helpless, God is on the job. He can be trusted.*

So each week had a new beginning. Drop the kids off at school and head to church for some needed support on Monday mornings.

The first time the group got together Pastor Graff read from Exodus chapter six, *"God said to Moses, 'I am the Lord...I have heard the groaning of the Israelites, whom the Egyptians are enslaving, and I have remembered my covenant. Therefore, say to the Israelites: "I am the Lord, and I will bring you out from under the yoke of the Egyptians. I will free you from being slaves to them, and I will redeem you with an outstretched arm"""(vss.2,5-6).*

Even when we are helpless, God is on the job. He can be trusted.

That was the strength Mr. Thorpe needed, especially for the next decision that had to be made. After six weeks and job prospects that were slim to none, Mrs. Thorpe suggested that she get a part-time job. This was not in the plan. They prayed about it and agreed to give it a try. It didn't take long for Mrs. Thorpe to find a part-time position assisting the pharmacist at the new Rite-Aid drug store in town.

"Oh, the depth of the riches of the wisdom and knowledge of God! How unsearchable his judgments, and his paths beyond tracing out!" The search went on. Life was changing. But through it all, the Lord, the Savior with His outstretched arm, was still on the job.

Devotion/Study Guide for chapter 13: On the Job

Discuss:

Read Romans 8:22-34

According to these verses, who is helping us when we are in trouble?

What struggles do you think Mr. Thorpe was facing in his new situation of being jobless?

How have you seen God on the job in your life when things aren't going the way you expected them to?

Apply:

Read verse 32 of Romans chapter 8. Talk about what it means for your life.

Pray:

Pray for three people in your life who need to know and see that God is on the job.

Tackling Issues
To Be a Family
Chapter Fourteen

"Open my eyes that I may see..." Psalm 119:18

T he Rite-Aid Pharmacy was not a bad place to work. Except on Tuesdays. That's when an out-of-town substitute pharmacist filled in for Mrs. Thorpe's regular boss. The substitute was not a very sociable man, and Mrs. Thorpe questioned his genuine interest in the customer. One woman from Harrison came into the store with a reply to a dinner invitation that she had sent out. The person she invited was a doctor. He sent back a reply, but the woman could not read the handwriting to find out whether or not the doctor was coming. So the woman asked Mrs. Thorpe if she thought the pharmacist could decipher the doctor's handwriting—that's something that many pharmacists seemed to master.

It was Tuesday. Mrs. Thorpe approached the substitute pharmacist and asked, "Could you read this for a customer who just came in?"

The pharmacist looked at the scrawl carefully and stepped to the back of his work area. A few minutes later he returned with a small bottle of medicine, handed it to the woman and said, "That will be twenty-two dollars."

Apparently he was seeing more than there really was.

Mr. Thorpe, however, thought he was seeing very clearly. After being out of work for over four months, after going through the frustration of a slow job market in the Harrison area, after sending out resumes, making phone calls, praying, reading the Bible—after hanging on, Mr. Thorpe finally had a lead. And he really thought that this could be it.

A major manufacturing company wrote back to Mr. Thorpe letting him know that they were interested in his qualifications and would like to set up an interview. The opportunity looked fantastic. He would have to break the news gently to his family, though. You see, the company was in Texas. But maybe some sacrifices would have to be made. You can't always be comfortable, Mr. Thorpe thought.

That evening Mr. Thorpe talked to his wife about the new possibility.

She shared her husband's excitement, but was honest when she asked, "Do you really think Texas is for us?"

Mr. Thorpe said, "I think I need to take a look at this. It's been over four months. It might have to be an option."

When Mr. and Mrs. Thorpe let the children know about the interview in Texas, Ernest was the most vocal. "Yes! Texas!" he said. "Let's go! I'm going to get me a cowboy hat. Warm weather, here I come! Shorts in January! Goodbye snow, hello sun! Goodbye Detroit Lions, hello Dallas Cowboys! Dad, it feels right. Let's go."

That week Ernest started telling his friends that he was going to move to Texas. Oil wells, cattle ranches, the land of prosperity, Ernest told them. There would probably be an in-ground swimming pool at his new house, he told Paul Tucker. "And you should see those Texas girls," Ernest added with a big smile at Paul.

Perhaps Ernest was seeing more than there really was.

Mr. Thorpe flew down for his first interview. What a report he brought back! What a company! And what a place to live! They needed a guy just like him. The money looked great. The benefits were fantastic. They could live in a major suburban area with shopping malls all over the place—anything you wanted at your finger-tips. He would be heading up one of the production facilities for gaming equipment—slot machines and other casino supplies. The market was booming and this company was riding the wave. There would be lots of hours. It was a three shift, six day a week operation. And there would be travel. But, what an opportunity!

Mrs. Thorpe tried her best to be objective as she listened to the details. As they sat in the family room, energy filled the place. Mr. Thorpe had a packet of housing information and colorful chamber of commerce brochures that he spread out on the table. Karen was looking at the mall pamphlets. James was trying to slide some business cards from realtors into the DVD player. And Ernest kept singing, "Texas is the place I really want to be!"

Mrs. Thorpe was listening and was trying to ask some questions. This was a major family decision. This was a major LIFE decision! Mrs. Thorpe kept trying to restrain James, and Mr. Thorpe kept asking Ernest to be quiet. But Ernest kept singing and singing and singing. Then James started to yell because he was being stopped from accomplishing his mission. Finally Mr. Thorpe had enough.

"Ernest! That's enough! Get out of here!" Mr. Thorpe yelled. He nearly shoved his son out of the room and told everyone else to be quiet. Karen started crying and ran to her room. James hugged his mom. Mrs. Thorpe stared at her husband in disbelief.

"They want me to come down for a second interview. I'm leaving in the morning. This is too important to mess around with." Mr. Thorpe stormed out and started packing.

Mr. Thorpe was experiencing one of those times when you get totally out of sync as an individual and as a family. You just can't see clearly. After the damage is done you wish you could start all over. But it seems very complicated to do that. Feeling out of sorts, Mr. Thorpe went to the airport and caught his flight to Texas.

The second interview took place right after Mr. Thorpe arrived in Texas. His luggage was still in the limousine as he talked with more upper management types. Once again, the interview was a major success. Before he left the office, Mr. Thorpe was offered the job. He couldn't believe it. Finally, relief! Finally, employment! Finally, someone wanted him.

The limo took Mr. Thorpe to his hotel. He checked in, went to his room and opened his suitcase. Inside was a note on a piece of pink stationery. It was from his wife. It had a quote written first: *"Arise, shine, for your light has come, and the glory of the Lord rises upon you. See, darkness covers the earth and thick darkness is over the peoples, but the Lord rises upon you and his glory appears over you. Nations will come to your light, and kings to the brightness of your dawn"(Isaiah 60:1-3).*

Then Mrs. Thorpe had written: "If this is the light of Christ out of our darkness, I will go with you. I love you always."

Was this job the light of Christ? Was God in this? Was this right? The devil sure got a hold of their family discussion, Mr. Thorpe thought. That was terrible. He was so wrong. Now what? Mr. Thorpe thought and prayed. What did he see? What did he really see? Could the light of Christ pierce the thick darkness Mr. Thorpe was experiencing?

Mr. Thorpe picked up the phone and called a Christian friend of his from back home. He told his friend about the job, the money, the opportunity, the hours, the travel, and the gaming business. And he told his friend about the family strife. He needed to get an objective opinion. Mr. Thorpe's friend listened carefully.

"I think you just told me your answer," he said to Mr. Thorpe. "It doesn't sound like you're convinced that the job would be good for you, for your family, or for what you're contributing to society as a follower of Christ."

This was a tough one. But making decisions, choosing actions that follow and honor Christ are not always easy. Mr. Thorpe knew that it was time for him to head home from Texas with apologies, in humility, and without a job. It was still time to wait. It was important to be a family.

Devotion/Study Guide for chapter 14: To be a Family

Discuss:

Read Ephesians 3:8-11

Why do you need God's wisdom?

What difference does it make in your decisions?

What finally convinced Mr. Thorpe to make the decision he did? Evaluate each factor to see if it is part of your life.

Read Ephesians 1:17-23

What family life choices have you made or are you making?

How can knowing the Lord Jesus better help you in those decisions?

Apply:

Read Romans 12:1-2

Use the next twenty-four hours to think and pray about what it means to be a living sacrifice to God—to live a life of worship in all you do and with all the people in your life.

Pray:

Ask God to guide you in a decision you are thinking about. Thank Him for shining His light into your life.

Tackling Issues
To Be a Friend
Chapter Fifteen

Jesus said, "I have called you friends." John 15:15

Y ou don't always know what's really going on in someone's life by outward appearances, do you? The same was true for the Thorpe family from the small town of Harrison, Michigan. Life looked just like many other lives look: There were diapers for the baby; school, homework and Brownies for their 3rd grade daughter; and a busy high school life for son Ernest. Mr. and Mrs. Thorpe did mom and dad things. The days were full.

But as is usually the case for every individual and every family, there was much more going on inside. In spite of the outward appearance, the Thorpe family was a family going through adversity.

They were beginning to adjust to the job search mode, but as time went on, Mr. and Mrs. Thorpe noticed some subtle changes taking place. Some of their friends had become very scarce. They weren't around anymore. They didn't call like they used to. Maybe they didn't know what to say. Maybe they felt awkward about Mr. Thorpe's ongoing unemployment. Perhaps they were busy with all that life brought. But Mr. and Mrs. Thorpe felt a strange sense of loneliness and loss in the midst of their crisis. Were they being a burden? They didn't have all the answers, but they did have some wounds.

The Thorpe children didn't seem to pick up on the undercurrent of sadness that their parents were experiencing. In fact, Ernest was riding a wave of new friendship opportunities. He was driving for about six months now. So were plenty of his friends. That opened up a new world of social adventure! This was high school, and Saturday nights took on a whole new meaning. It was party time!

Andy Oreby was going to pick up Ernest and Paul Tucker for a party over at Stephanie Revin's house. It sounded like everybody was going to be there. Andy swung by Ernest's place at eight-o'clock. Paul was already in the car. The radio was blasting, the windows were rolled down—they didn't even care that it was winter! Three sixteen-year-olds were out on the town! They were laughing, joking and feeling free! They were friends.

Andy told Ernest and Paul to stay out of his way at the party. He was going to try to get to know Amanda Leeland and he didn't want any interference. Ernest thought Amanda was very nice.

"All right, Andy," Ernest said.

Paul chimed in, "I thought I smelled a little cologne on you. I thought you were trying to impress us!"

The threesome laughed all the way to Stephanie Revin's house.

Stephanie's house was packed. She lived out in the country and cars lined the road. Even though the weather was chilly, there were even people standing outside. It looked like everyone was having fun. Andy went off on his own in search of

114

Amanda Leeland. Ernest and Paul got some munchies, talked to some friends, and listened to the music. It was a great time. Everyone was having fun together. It was great to be with friends!

As time passed, Ernest and Paul noticed that they didn't see Stephanie's parents around. But they did start seeing beer and wine. All through his years of growing up Ernest heard all about the danger of peer pressure. He was taught at home. He was given facts at school. There were open discussions about drug and alcohol abuse. Everyone at the party had heard all of that too. They had final exams that dealt with alcohol facts. The knowledge was there.

But everyone was having fun. There was laughter and music. People weren't just walking by each other in the hallways like they had to do at school. They were talking, getting to know each other, and interested in each other! Knowledge wasn't the issue. This was an event. This was the flow of being together, of being friends. Parents' warnings, school lessons, and confirmation class teachings were the farthest things from Ernest's mind. Nothing bad seemed to be happening. This was friendship and fun.

Meanwhile, back at home, Mr. and Mrs. Thorpe were having a quiet evening together. James and Karen were asleep. But Mr. and Mrs. Thorpe didn't feel very settled inside. They were feeling sad. True, it was great for them to be together. If they discovered anything during this time of adversity, it was that they were each other's friends. This experience definitely brought them closer. It also brought them closer to some very caring friends at church. But still, what about the others? Even some people in their own family seemed to be turning their backs on them. Just because they were different now, they were being left alone.

That's when the doorbell rang. Right when they were in the middle of another conversation about this strange hurt, Josh Dale appeared at the door. Ever since Mrs. Thorpe invited Josh and his daughter Lisa to church for Christmas Eve, and since both of them lost their jobs, Mr. Dale and Mr. Thorpe had been getting together regularly. Josh was smiling and holding a pizza box in his hand.

"With the big party going on," he said, "I thought I'd risk a pizza run. How 'bout it?"

The Thorpe's smiled and ushered Josh into the house. It was good to get a boost from a friend.

At Stephanie Revin's house, it took a couple of hours before Ernest and Paul decided to find the cooler with the beer in it. They dug into the ice, pulled out the cans and were just about to open them when they heard laughter by the living room window. Some kids were pointing outside to the front lawn.

"Look at Oreby!" some of them said.

Ernest and Paul inched into the crowd so they could see what everyone was laughing at.

They were shocked to see Andy lying on the ground face down. Both Ernest and Paul pushed their way out of the living room, tossed their unopened beer cans back into the cooler and ran out the front door to Andy. People were standing around him and laughing. Apparently Andy got caught up in the party atmosphere pretty quickly. Andy was drunk. He was nearly unconscious. It was cold outside and he was sprawled flat on the ground without a coat. His head was resting in the place where he had thrown up. It

116

was terrible. Andy was so drunk that he even wet his pants. He had totally lost control. And everyone just stood there laughing. This was not fun and friendship.

Ernest and Paul helped Andy up. They took him into the house. Once inside, they brought him into the kitchen, sat him down at the kitchen table, and cleaned him up as best they could.

Andy kept crying and speaking nonsense: "No one loves me. No one cares," he moaned. "I couldn't find Amanda. I'm glad she can't see me now."

Ernest looked out of the corner of his eye and saw Amanda Leeland watching this episode. Paul got Andy's coat for him. Ernest took the car keys. Now they had the difficult task of driving Andy home. What would his parents say?

Ernest and Paul buckled Andy into the car. The ride home from Stephanie Revin's was a lot quieter than the ride there. Ernest knew that everyone at that party studied what he had studied in school. They knew all the facts. But too many of them would be driving home with drinks in them. Too many would be going with the flow. They were being taken captive by the moment and were ignoring what being a friend really is.

"How did I get so close to buying into that?" Ernest thought to himself. Ernest wondered how long it would take for Andy's parents to trust him again. He also wondered how long all those friends would have let Andy lay there.

It was about 11:15 in the evening when Ernest and Paul explained to Mr. and Mrs. Oreby what happened. Andy's folks were visibly shaken. Mr. Oreby drove Paul and Ernest home. He thanked them for being Andy's friends.

Ernest's parents were surprised to see Ernest home a half hour before his curfew. He came in and told the whole story to his parents. It looked like Andy would be okay, he said. Mr. and Mrs. Thorpe thanked their son for his honesty. Ernest said good-night and went to bed.

> *Jesus didn't just stand on the sidelines and laugh at our plight. He gave His life for us.*

The next morning Ernest's family sat together in church and listened to verses from the book of Isaiah in the Bible. Pastor Graff read, *"I will take hold of your hand...to open the eyes that are blind, to free captives...to release from the dungeon those who sit in darkness."*

That sounded like a friend. It was the Savior God who cared and went into action by sending His Son, Jesus. And Jesus didn't just stand on the sidelines and laugh at our plight. He gave His life for us. Every day He still picks us up, cleans us up from our sins, helps us, and sticks with us all the way through life to life in heaven. Pastor Graff said it well when he quoted 2 Corinthians 4:8-9, *"We are often troubled, but not crushed; sometimes in doubt, but never in despair; there are many enemies, but we are never without a friend."*

Mr. and Mrs. Thorpe and Ernest saw again that there is a big difference between getting caught up in the flow of what's going on and being a real friend. That morning, once again, they knew that they were taken by the hand and led by the One who is their friend, their true friend. He is exactly the One they needed.

Jesus made the decision to be that. And making the decision to really care and do something about it was what the Thorpe family was ready to do, too. It takes time and patience. It means risking being unselfish and different. It involves feeling something and doing something for the people in your life. And it all comes from one important decision: the decision to be a friend.

Devotion/Study Guide for chapter 15: To be a Friend

Discuss:

Read John 15:12-13

How does Jesus qualify for being your friend?

Tell your family (take turns) or a friend how Jesus has been your friend during a specific time of your life.

Read Ephesians 4:29 - 5:2

What qualities of friendship do you see in these verses?

Talk about who showed these qualities and who didn't in the story.

How can you grow in those qualities?

Apply:

Read Galatians 6:2

Do you know someone who is bearing a burden? Today, pray for them and contact them so you can help share their burden.

Pray:

Thank Jesus for being your friend. Ask Him to help grow you in two specific qualities of friendship.

To Really Love
Chapter Sixteen

"Love is patient, love is kind. It does not envy, it does not boast, it is not proud.

It is not rude, it is not self-seeking, it is not easily angered, it keeps no record of wrongs.

Love does not delight in evil but rejoices with the truth.

It always protects, always trusts, always hopes, always perseveres.

Love never fails."

1 Corinthians 13:4-8

I f you have ever experienced life in a small town, you know that choices of where to go and what to do are limited. And, if you were planning a big date in Harrison, being limited is not exactly what you would want. Where's the best place to go according to some of the high school crowd? "Out of town" is their recommendation.

Ernest Thorpe was trying to follow that advice. He was planning a big date—out of town. A good movie was playing in Clare. There was a good pizza place there. It sounded like a good plan. And Allison Iverson was the girl he wanted to ask out. The movie and pizza choices were easy. The "asking the girl" part of this date was where Ernest experienced some hesitation. He couldn't ask her at school. Too many of her friends were always around her and too many of Ernest's friends would give him a hard time. The phone was no good. It made Ernest too nervous, and he wanted to see Allison's face when he asked her. He couldn't just go over to her house—that would be way too daring! How was Ernest going to ask Allison Iverson out for a date? Ernest was wishing that there were some books on this subject in the library. Why didn't they teach a class about this in school?

"I'd sure be able to use that more than advanced math," Ernest thought.

Then Ernest had an idea. Right after school was out he would stop Allison on the sidewalk before she got to her bus. Both sets of their friends would be dispersed, and in the confusion of school getting out, all he would have to do was to stop her and speak to her face to face. Okay, that wasn't such an easy part, but Ernest was ready to take that chance.

The final bell of the day echoed through the Harrison High School hallways. Ernest saw Allison getting ready to walk to the bus. She was beautiful. Long blond hair hung to the middle of her back. Her face lit up when she smiled. She laughed when Ernest said something funny. And when Ernest sat behind her in physics class, he couldn't stop breathing in her good smell.

It was time. Ernest's heart was pounding. He was glad he had a coat on because he was sure his sweat was soaking right into his shirt. "Just look cool, look happy," Ernest said to himself.

He caught up with Allison. "Allison!" Ernest called out. "Hi!"

"Hi Ernest." Allison said it with a smile.

No immediate rejection. That was a good sign.

"How would you like to go out Friday night?" Ernest asked. "I was thinking about a movie down in Clare and some pizza." He said it. He asked. And it sounded pretty normal.

Allison responded: "That sounds nice, Ernest. Call me and let me know what time you want to pick me up."

"Great!" Ernest said. "I'll call you."

Off Allison went. Wow! That went okay. It took a few years off Ernest's life, but it went okay—even though he still ended up with having to make a phone call!

"There's got to be a better way to do this," Ernest mumbled. But at least Allison agreed. He was going out with Allison Iverson on Friday night!

Ernest went home and asked his mom and dad about the car again. "I can still use the car on Friday night, can't I?"

"Did you ask Allison out?" Mrs. Thorpe asked.

"Oh yeah," Ernest replied. "I asked her out. No problem. I've got to call her now."

Mr. Thorpe walked over to his wife and put his arm around her. "We guys have all the hard work. That's why we don't live as long. It's the dating thing that takes the years off early."

Mrs. Thorpe rolled her eyes. "Ernest, I hope you have a nice time with Allison," Mrs. Thorpe said.

Karen, who just happened to be listening in on the conversation, walked into the room and said, "Ernest and Allison sitting in a tree K-I-S-S-I-N-G!"

"Karen," Ernest said, "We're just going on a date. We're not going to be K-I-S-S-I-N-G."

"I don't think so," Karen answered.

Ernest wondered if there was a plot against him.

Somehow word got around school that Ernest was going to go out with Allison. Ernest's friends showed no mercy.

"Hey Ernest," Paul Tucker started out, "Allison Iverson— good choice! Give us the report after Friday."

"Yeah," another friend chimed in, "We want to know how far you got with her."

"Hot date, Ernest," another boy said, "A hot date!"

Ernest tried to smile as the group was walking away, but he was angry. All everyone was talking about boiled down to sex! Sure, Allison was beautiful. Ernest liked her. He wanted to talk to her and get to know her. But he wasn't thinking about sex! What was going on?

When Ernest got home his mom was at work already. Ernest's dad was looking through the newspapers for job leads.

Ernest sat at the table with his dad and asked him, "Dad, all I'm getting from my friends about my date on Friday is talk about how far I'm going to get with Allison and stuff like that. Even Karen is just thinking about 'making out.' What problem does everyone have with a date?"

"There's a big problem, Ernest," his father replied. "The world says that if you put a man and a woman together it means either fighting or sex. Look at TV. Think about the ads you see in magazines or on billboards. What gets left out is LOVE. And I don't mean 'falling in love.' I mean respect, honor, joy and friendship. It's disappearing.

> *"What gets left out is LOVE. And I don't mean 'falling in love.' I mean respect, honor, joy, and friendship."*

When I was your age I could go on a date. Sure, there were some jokes. But nowadays a girl and boy can hardly be friends. You don't get to know each other. There's too much pressure that being together means sex."

"Well, what can I do?" Ernest asked.

Mr. Thorpe picked up his Bible that was by his newspapers. "You can be an honorable young man," he said.

Then he read: *"Flee from sexual immorality. All other sins a man commits are outside his body, but he who sins sexually sins against his own body. Do you not know that your body is a temple of the Holy Spirit, who is in you, whom you have received from God? You are not your own, you were bought at a price. Therefore honor God with your body"(1 Corinthians 6:18-20).*

Mr. Thorpe continued. "You can honor God and every girl you go out with, Ernest. Sex can honor God or dishonor Him. You can respect sex as God's gift for marriage, or you can misuse sex. But Jesus bought you with His life and death, and made you a new creation. You don't have to get stuck in the way the world goes. Forgiveness means new beginnings. Just follow God. Be a leader to honor Him and your date. And have fun."

Have fun. No one mentioned that. Why did everyone forget? Ernest was glad that his dad took the pressure off. And fun would be easy to have with a nice girl like Allison Iverson.

Ernest made the phone call to Allison and took care of the arrangements. Friday night arrived and they had a great time. They enjoyed themselves. And when Ernest's friends asked about it, Ernest said, "We had fun." He was telling the truth.

Ernest made the decision to really love—to be giving, caring, polite and unselfish. There was no pressure and there were no games. Allison thought it was very nice.

Mr. Thorpe passed on to his son another part of the new life Jesus gives. It's a good part, too. He lets you really love.

Devotion/Study Guide for chapter 16: To Really Love

Discuss:

Read 1 John 4:7-11

What is love? How is God's definition different from the world's?

What important lesson did Ernest learn about dating and relationships?

Read 1 Corinthians 6:18-20

How do these verses give guidance about honoring God with your body?

How do you do that as a single person and as a married person?

How can you honor God with your body in other areas of life?

Apply:

Read Hebrews 10:24-25

What is a key ingredient to learning how to really love? Tell someone (take turns in your family) how getting together with fellow Christians helps you to live a God-honoring life.

Pray:

Ask God to give you strength and self-control as you seek to live in honor and purity.

Tackling Issues
To Be Faithful
Chapter Seventeen

"Many a man claims to have unfailing love, but a faithful man who can find?" Proverbs 20:6

A little over six years ago life was sailing along for Mr. Joshua Dale. He lived in Harrison, Michigan and operated his own carpentry business there. He had a beautiful wife and a lovely daughter. Mr. Dale was doing well. He loved his work, and he was glad about his success. He wanted to provide for his family and make sure they weren't just scraping by. The more work he did, the more phone calls he got lining up new jobs. People praised his craftsmanship. He had a reputation for quality. So he kept taking on more and more work. It was not uncommon for him to get up at four in the morning to head to the office. It became a regular routine for him to come home at ten at night after tackling several jobs—paperwork included. He crammed in every job he could on weekends, too. After all, people needed him.

It all happened very slowly, but it wasn't long before work took over Josh Dale's life. It was in the middle of this frenzy of prosperity that the unexpected happened. Mrs. Dale was diagnosed with cancer. The diagnosis came out of the blue. Cancer wasn't in the family. Mrs. Dale didn't smoke. The risk factors in her life were very low. But the discovery of cancer set in motion a two year battle with the illness. There were surgeries, chemotherapy and radiation treatments, times of hospitalization, and all of the ups and downs, the good outlooks and the dashed hopes, that sometimes come with cancer. But after two years the cancer won. Josh Dale's wife died.

Mr. Dale didn't slow down. He just got bitter. He turned into the guy who drives behind you and lets you know that you're not going fast enough—he's got someplace to be. He took the use of foul language to a new extreme—it didn't matter who was around. He argued about trivia, but he always had to prove a point. He didn't communicate; he talked. And his daughter, Lisa, went from having an absentee father to having an angry absentee father. It broke Lisa's heart that everything was important to her father except what really mattered. He didn't seem to think about her mother anymore. Even Lisa felt abandoned to deal with her sadness all by herself. Her father's rage was so loud and so constant, however, she could hardly even manage to do that.

Josh Dale's life was crumbling and it began to show in his business. He was losing customers, losing referrals, and losing money. Life was going downhill fast.

That's when, out of the blue one day, he received a note from Mrs. Thorpe. Her son Ernest was a classmate of Lisa. Josh had done some work for the Thorpe's after Ernest, who was just learning to drive, crashed into the garage door. Mrs. Thorpe wrote about how she had lost someone very dear to her, too. She also wrote about being mended in her soul. She invited Mr. Dale and Lisa to come to Christmas Eve worship with them. It had been a long time since he'd been in church. But at that time in Josh Dale's life, he was beginning to sense that he needed some mending in his soul. So Josh and Lisa joined the Thorpe's that Christmas Eve.

As they sat in church, Mr. Dale sensed that there was something very different going on. He wasn't hearing the same old Christmas story. The same words were being read, but he was hearing something more. He heard about God who gave His all so that He could be close to us again.

"That's how much He loves you," the pastor said.

Mr. Dale thought about how he would give anything just to embrace his wife again, just to be close to her again.

"That's how much God loves you." The words rang in his ears.

At that moment in time, Mr. Dale felt like he could feel the feelings of God, the desire of one who loves to be close to his beloved.

"Could it be true for me?" Josh Dale thought. "Is that how God feels about me?"

Then he heard a line of a song: "The hopes and fears of all the years are met in Thee tonight."

Was this the time and place that the turmoil of Josh Dale's life would be taken in hand by someone who cared, by someone who could really help? Could Jesus carry his hopes and fears?

For the first time in a long time Josh Dale prayed. "God, let it be true," he said.

The service ended. Mr. Dale and his daughter thanked the Thorpe's before heading home. The ride home was quiet, but Mr. Dale's thoughts were anything but silent. Would Jesus step into his life to carry his hopes and fears? Mr. Dale was going to wait and see.

> *A sense of hope and excitement filled him when he realized that he would be able to see her again in heaven.*

After the first of the year, Josh Dale's business had nearly come to a halt. It was then that Mr. Thorpe invited him to join in some Bible reading and praying on Mondays. Josh agreed.

"Maybe this is the beginning," he thought.

Slowly Josh Dale discovered the Good News of God for His hopes and fears. He grew to understand the hope his wife had as she faced death. He realized why she insisted that the cancer did not win. A sense of hope and excitement filled him when he realized that he would be able to see her again in heaven. He didn't quite know how it was happening, but he could sense that a mending of his soul was going on. It was just like Mrs. Thorpe described in her letter. And to Josh, it felt so good not to be alone anymore.

132

Josh Dale started to wonder how he could have wasted so much time. He realized that even in the midst of running away and isolating himself, God still valued his life—his bitter, profane, and distracted life. God gave it all—His only Son Jesus, so he could be brought close.

Josh thought to himself, "So what am I doing? If God has done all this for me and life is this precious, what am I doing for the lives around me? What am I doing that is really important?"

Josh Dale started answering the question. What better place to start than with the people in his own life? Josh was still spending a lot of time at his office. But on Tuesdays he changed his routine. Around 11:30 in the morning he got in his truck and drove down to Clare. His wife's grandma was in the nursing care center there. Josh and his wife used to always go and visit with grandma. Now, after a few years, Josh and grandma were getting reacquainted. They ate lunch. They talked. They shared some unresolved grief. They even sat and watched TV for a little while. Josh gave grandma a hug and a kiss before he left.

"I've been praying for you," grandma whispered.

"Thank you," Josh whispered back.

Josh wondered about his friends, too. He really didn't have any. He used to, but he had done a very thorough job in driving everyone out of his life. But the Thorpe's had reached out to him. And he was meeting with Mr. Thorpe regularly as they both were struggling with the loss of work. One evening while his daughter was at a big party with kids from school, Josh bought a pizza and brought it over to the Thorpe's house. They had a nice evening together. It was a little surprise that seemed to lift their spirits. It was an act of friendship. And that was important.

Then there was Lisa, Josh's daughter. She had been bearing the brunt of his lost life for these six years. He loved her, but the pathway he was on was leading him further and further away from her. So after that Christmas Eve service, Mr. Dale put his wife's picture back in the living room and he sat with his daughter and told every story he could think of about her mother. They laughed and they cried, together. And Lisa was thrilled.

Mr. Dale could tell that Lisa was very tentative about this change in his life. But he was going to let her know that this was important and it was here to stay. After the Christmas decorations were down at home and Lisa seemed to be feeling a little sad, Mr. Dale decided to come home early from his office and surprise his daughter. He walked through the doorway of the house with a fistful of flowers and said, "These are for you. It was looking a little dreary in here. I wanted to let you know that not all the beautiful things are gone."

What a smile Lisa had. Not all the beautiful things were gone! It was important to know that. For the first time in a long time Lisa felt like she was important to her father.

In the evening Mr. Dale started doing something he had never done before. He sat quietly to read the Bible and to think and pray it into his life. He never wanted to do that before because he didn't want to think about his life at all. Now he read, *"If anyone is in Christ, he is a new creation; the old has gone, the new has come!"(2 Corinthians 5:17)* It was time to think about his life. Before, he could barely stand the thought of another day, but now Mr. Dale could think about his life as one that was not alone, and as one that had hope.

When that quiet time was finished, Mr. Dale got ready for bed. He looked in on Lisa as she was sleeping. She looked like an angel. He used to look at her and feel only guilt. Now he knew that it wasn't guilt he felt anymore. He felt hope. He felt like he had a call in life. It was a call to do what was most important. It was a call to follow in the footsteps of Jesus. It was a call to treasure lives. It was a call TO BE FAITHFUL.

Devotion/Study Guide for chapter 17: To be Faithful

Discuss:

Read Colossians 3:12-17

TO BE FAITHFUL WITH GOD: What is important to do in your relationship with God? What did Mr. Dale discover?

Read Isaiah 30:15

TO BE FAITHFUL WITH YOUR SELF: What is important to do for your own well-being?

How does the verse above describe God's desire for your personal health and well-being?

Why does He want that for you?

Apply:

Read 1 Timothy 5:7-8

TO BE FAITHFUL WITH YOUR FAMILY: How do you provide for your fellow family members faithfully? What do you need to provide them with? How can you do that better?

Pray:

Ask God for some specific blessings in your relationship with Him, with yourself, with your family, and with your friends.

Building Trust

Giving Thanks

Chapter Eighteen

"Sing and make music in your heart to the Lord, always giving thanks to God the Father for everything, in the name of our Lord Jesus Christ" Ephesians 5:19-20.

L ately Mr. Thorpe felt like he did a few years back when he had the opportunity to take a cow for a walk. That's right, a COW. Gidget was a 2-month-old little cow. As Mr. Thorpe admired her in the cow barn at the county fair, the owner said, "Would you like to take her for a walk? She really could use the exercise."

So he did. And a funny thing happens when you're walking a cow around a barn. People think you're a cow expert. If you saw someone walking a cow around, you'd probably think that the person knew what he was doing. Well, people thought that about Mr. Thorpe. They started asking questions:

"How old is this cow?"

"What's her name?"

Of course, Mr. Thorpe could answer. He just got the full scoop of information from the owner of the cow. So, as Mr. Thorpe engaged in some in-depth conversation with the many cow admirers who gathered around him, Mrs. Thorpe tried to contain her laughter. Here was a person who didn't even like milk all that much looking like a cow expert.

But just because someone's hanging on to a cow doesn't mean he's a cow expert. It's the same with a lot of situations in life. Just because you're going through it doesn't mean that you're an expert. Adversity, for instance. Is anyone an expert when it comes to hard times?

That was the situation that Mr. Thorpe was in. He was hanging on to something that he was no expert in. He was out of a job. It had been a year now. This was a time of adversity. Financially, it was crushing. Ernest would be starting college in one year, but now the college fund was gone. The family was barely making it. If Mrs. Thorpe didn't have her job at the pharmacy, they would not be making it at all. Morale was at a low point for Mr. Thorpe. He felt lousy. So many efforts seemed to be in vain. He was trying and trying and trying, but nothing was working. He had become an expert in laundry, potty training, and grocery shopping. But he didn't want to be! And his faith—he felt it was on shaky ground. Even though he had been praying and reading the Bible more than ever, he just couldn't figure out what God was doing.

And then, on a sunny August day, Mr. Thorpe got a phone call. A year after the factory closed down, it was opening again. Another company had purchased the business. The plan was to expand. And they needed Mr. Thorpe. On Monday!

Just like that Mr. Thorpe had a job again. He called his wife. Both of them were thrilled! It was amazing! It made no sense at all. Who could ever be an expert through events like these?

But before Mr. Thorpe could get too excited, he had some business to take care of. His wife wanted him to drop off some prescriptions at the nursing home, and he had to stop at Ashcraft's supermarket for a few groceries.

Mr. Thorpe walked into the nursing home. It was not one of those new kinds of nursing homes. It was old and plain and noisy. It didn't smell very clean. But it was a familiar place for Mr. Thorpe. Throughout his year of unemployment he stopped at the nursing home regularly to deliver prescriptions for the pharmacy. Mr. Thorpe usually dropped off the medication, walked around and greeted residents, sat and chatted with a few, and helped himself to some of the cookies at the front desk. As the months went by Mr. Thorpe started to deliver other items that residents requested. When he had a morning delivery he would bring in fresh coffee. Sometimes he would share a basket of raspberries that were just picked from his garden. He had Charlie's electric razor repaired and he lubed Mrs. Joan's wheelchair.

Today he was bringing a newspaper to Ann. Ann was in her upper eighties. She had no family left. Her body was not a friend to her anymore. Health problems were coming one after another. But a visit from Mr. Thorpe usually brought a smile to her face. Ann forgot her pain and loneliness for a little while as she visited with her new friend.

"I got my job back today, Ann," Mr. Thorpe said.

"Congratulations," Ann replied. "It's been a hard year."

Mr. Thorpe nodded in agreement.

"But all you can do," Ann said, "is to go through it. Go through it with Jesus."

Ann put her head back on her pillow and closed her eyes.

Adversity. It's tiring, numbing, draining, depressing. It's the long haul of life. You may be an expert at experiencing adversity, but getting through it—that's another story.

As Mr. Thorpe looked at Ann, he wondered, "Why?" Why? Why? Why?

That's when he saw the two pictures above Ann's bed. He never noticed them before. Ann had never napped while he was in her room. This time he saw the pictures. One was of Jesus kneeling in prayer in the garden of Gethsemane. He was in agony. Tiring, numbing, draining, depressing adversity. It was the long haul of life. The picture captured what Jesus was going through on the evening before the cross. Mr. Thorpe looked at Him, all alone. There was Jesus, going through adversity for us. Mr. Thorpe recalled that Jesus even asked "Why?"

"My God, my God, why have you forsaken me?"
(Matthew 27:46)

That's what Jesus said on the cross. It's the question that adversity brings. It's the question Mr. Thorpe had to fight as he went through this year of unemployment. It may be a question you wrestle with in your adversity, too. But in that picture Mr. Thorpe saw again what Jesus did. He came and *"took sin down with Him,"* and brought God Himself down to us *(the Message, Romans 6:10).* You're not forsaken. Through Jesus, God gives life and hope and strength and help in the midst of adversity. And one day the adversity will be over.

It was in the picture.

Jesus brings an answer to adversity. Not always to the question "Why?" but always to the question, "What?"—"What will I do now?"

> *Through Jesus, God gives life and hope and strength and help in the midst of adversity.*

Jesus answers, "Here I am to go through it with you."

Through Jesus, His Son, God became an expert in adversity.

The second picture was an artistic drawing of words from Ephesians 5, *"Sing and make music in your heart to the Lord, always giving thanks to God the Father for everything, in the name of our Lord Jesus Christ"(Ephesians 5:19-20).*

Sing? Always giving thanks? If the first picture wasn't there this would make no sense at all. But Mr. Thorpe realized that while he was not thankful for the adversity, he was thankful

141

that all of it took place while he was in Jesus Christ. That was something to sing about. With Jesus always with you, there was never a time not to give thanks.

Mr. Thorpe touched Ann's hand, whispered good-bye, and left the room. He went out to his car and opened his Bible to James chapter one. These are the words he read: *"Consider it a sheer gift, friends, when tests and challenges come at you from all sides. You know that under pressure, your faith-life is forced into the open and shows its true colors. So don't try to get out of anything prematurely. Let it do its work so you become mature and well-developed, not deficient in any way" (The Message, James 1:2-4).*

This year was a very strange gift for Mr. Thorpe. He wasn't able to call it a gift just yet. But he saw God with him through it. And for that he gave thanks.

Looking back was a lot easier than looking ahead. Having an answer was a lot easier than wondering what the answer might be. But through the good and the bad, God is faithful, and He does His good giving. That's what Mr. Thorpe saw God unfolding before him in Ann's room. That's what he saw as he started to look back at a turbulent year. Through it all was the good giving of God. Through it all was Jesus. He's the expert.

And He's hanging on to you.

Devotion/Study Guide for chapter 18: Giving Thanks

Discuss:

Read James 1:2-4

Think about times of adversity in your life. Have you grown in your faith because of those times? In what ways?

Read Romans 12:12

What do you see on either side of affliction in this verse?

How can these help you through adversity?

Apply:

Read Revelation 4:1-8

These verses give a picture of heaven. What significance is it that God is sitting on the throne? How does this impact your life that seems, at times, to be out of control?

Pray:

Pray through Psalm 136. Add your own thanks to this list.

Building Trust

Hanging Tough

Chapter Nineteen

"The LORD himself goes before you and will be with you; he will never leave you nor forsake you." Deuteronomy 31:8

It was an amazing experience when Mr. Thorpe and daughter Karen were able to go out on the sailboat together. It was Karen's first time sailing. Grandpa taught her about moving around on the trampoline of a catamaran, about watching the boom when there is a change in wind direction, and about operating the jib—the small sail in the front of the boat. So when she went out on the boat with her dad, she was all ready to go. It was a fairly calm day, and they went back and forth on Budd Lake. They even pulled the sails in all the way a few times and picked up some speed. Karen liked that the best. As they caught a good breeze and headed back home, Karen said to her dad, "Dad, I didn't know you knew how to sail. You're good at it."

Mr. Thorpe thanked her and thought, "Isn't it wonderful to be surprised by what someone knows and can do?"

Karen never would have known unless she went along with her father.

There is, however, an age in the learning curve when a person actually seems to know it all. When is that? Did you go through it? Maybe you are right now. For seventeen-year-old Ernest Thorpe in Harrison, Michigan, that was the case. He seemed to be beyond his parents' grasp of what was going on in life. In fact, he reminded them about that fact fairly often.

One area of life in which he seemed to surpass all knowledge and experience was that of automobiles. Ernest had been working hard all summer. With a residual $600 of earnings, Ernest had purchased a 1993 Ford F-150 pick-up truck. To Ernest Thorpe the vehicle was a thing of beauty. He waxed all the non-rusty spots. It had a sporadic shine as it rattled down the highway. It didn't have a sunroof, but there was an opening in the floorboards that let other elements of nature inside the cab. This was precious and hard earned transportation to a teen-age boy. Ernest Thorpe was in command of his mobility. And no one, no one, would interfere—including his father.

When Mr. Thorpe peeked under the hood after the purchase of this steed, Ernest promptly shooed him away and said, "Dad, I'll take care of it. I know it needs some work. I've got everything under control."

Ernest polished up the radiator cap and closed the hood. Mr. Thorpe tried to voice a suggestion, but was promptly silenced by the master mechanic who had climbed behind the wheel.

It was time to crank up this machine and enjoy an outing. Ernest and his friend, Paul Tucker, were going to see a movie in Clare. Clare was 13 miles away, and the master planners—Ernest and Paul—had a perfect strategy mapped out for the evening. They would arrive in Clare in time for the nine o'clock show, exit the movie theater at 10:45, grab some pizza at Bucilli's, start home at 11:45, and pull in the driveway at 11:58—two minutes before curfew! So off Ernest went, throwing into the driveway a few stones and a bit of dust from the back tires as he pulled out.

Everything went as planned for Ernest and Paul until they started to drive home. It was 11:47 when, suddenly, the truck engine died. Ernest coasted to the side of the road and turned on his hazard lights. The red tape over the tail lights allowed for quite a bright warning to other drivers—even though there were none.

In the sudden silence Ernest said to Paul, "Well, let's take a look under the hood."

Paul and Ernest got out of the truck and opened the engine compartment.

Paul said, "I can't see a thing. It's too dark."

Ernest dug an old penlight out of the glove compartment.

"Why don't we light a candle—maybe we'll get more light," Paul cracked.

"Be quiet and help me out," Ernest answered. "Hold this."

He handed the air cleaner cover to Paul.

"Why are you taking that off?" Paul asked.

By this time Ernest was getting frustrated. "I don't know," he said. "That's what you do when you look under the hood. You take the air cleaner cover off!"

"Are we out of gas?" Paul asked.

"No!" Ernest said. "I just filled it up."

"Maybe it leaked out." Paul added.

"Be quiet and try to start it," Ernest said.

Paul tried. It didn't start. Ernest stayed under the hood for a little while. All he succeeded in doing was to get a lot of grease on himself. Paul looked at the stars. Ernest looked into the darkness. Finally Ernest closed the hood. "Did you fix it?" Paul asked.

"No." Ernest answered. "Let's walk back to town. I've got to call my dad."

By the time they covered the two miles and called Mr. Thorpe it was 12:45. Mr. Thorpe just happened to be dressed and ready to go. He picked up the boys and drove back to the truck. Mr. Thorpe opened the hood, set up his portable trouble light, disconnected the wire to the distributor cap, and put a new one on.

"How did you know to bring that?" Ernest asked.

Mr. Thorpe told Ernest that he spotted the worn wire when he looked under the hood earlier that day. He knew it was just a matter of time and had purchased the wire replacement. He tried to tell Ernest before, but Ernest didn't want to listen.

All Ernest could say was, "Thanks dad."

Ernest was amazed at how much his dad knew and how much his dad could do. He was a good person to go to. Ernest was glad that his dad stuck with him.

As Mr. Thorpe drove home, he thought about the odyssey he had been going through. He remembered a devotion Pastor Graff had just led them through. It was from John chapter six and it resembled Mr. Thorpe's interaction with his son. Jesus was considered a meddler too. The people in John six knew it all. They were followers of Jesus, but didn't want Him looking under the hood of their lives. So when He said that without Him they would have no life in themselves (Jn. 6:53), they replied, "Well Jesus, what do you know?" And when He said *"The flesh counts for nothing" (Jn.6:63),--"A person's power is of no use at all,"* the people closed the hood and many of them left skid marks in the driveway. This Jesus was too inflexible, too narrow. He was too hard and difficult. It's hard to let someone else be in command of your mobility, isn't it? You shine up your rusty spots in life; you ignore your points of vulnerability; and you head out handling it all yourself. You and I want to be the master planners of our lives.

But even though Jesus knew that people would leave Him, He hung in there. He bought the parts we needed. He hung tough as He hung on the cross and purchased new life for you and me. He paid the price for our bad parts—our sin, and He arose from death to put us on the road of new life, life headed toward heaven.

> *Jesus hangs on to you. He hangs tough to carry your burdens and breakdowns.*

The people claimed that Jesus said hard things. The word in the Bible for "hard" is related to our word "skeleton." A skeleton is hard. It is tough. But it holds everything together, doesn't it? I don't know anyone who wants to get rid of his skeleton. That's why Peter said, *"Lord, to whom shall we go? You have the words of eternal life. We believe and know that you are the Holy One of God" (John 6:68-69).* Peter knew that it was only Jesus who could hang on to Him. It was only Jesus who could give him life.

And that Jesus hangs on to you. He hangs tough to carry your burdens and breakdowns. Who else could be so good to go to?

Sometimes it's such a surprise to see what a Father knows and what He can do. But you just don't know that unless you go along with Him.

Devotion/Study Guide for chapter 19: Hanging Tough

Discuss:

Read Psalm 31:1-5 (The whole Psalm if you have time)

How can you relate to this prayer?

How is your life different when it is in the Lord's hands?

What comfort or encouragement does this give you today?

Read Luke 23:44-46

Do you recognize these words of Jesus from the previous reading?

Why did Jesus speak these words?

When are you like Ernest—hesitant to ask for help?

What do these verses tell you about your place of refuge in adversity?

Apply:
Ask someone for help when you need it this week.

Pray:
Thank God for sticking with you when you were trying to go it alone.

Building Trust
Being Strong
Chapter Twenty

"Be strong in the Lord and in his mighty power."
Ephesians 6:10

H arrison is not all that different compared to other places in the world. True, the buildings are unique. They have a small town feel. The vegetation is definitely the type found in a northern Michigan lake community. But people are people. Life is life. During any given day in any given place people go through very similar ups and downs. People eat and drink, work and play, laugh and cry. People live life just one day at a time. And during the course of that day they need very similar things. Not just physical things like food and shoes and conversation and games to play. People need a life that is crafted in a way that will bring them to the next day as better people, stronger people, people with lives that are more complete.

God has a great way of giving those life-essentials on a daily basis. If you looked closely at any given day in any given place, you'd be able to see all those things showing up. Even if you took a look at a day in the life of Harrison, Michigan you would be able to spot them.

8:00 a.m. – Truth

At the home of the Thorpe family, little James was just over three years old. And he was a boy of truth. With his refined ability to speak the English language he called them as he saw them. At the end of the sermon in church he was the voice that asked, "Is he all done now?" He would announce his restroom needs in loud and graphic ways—it didn't matter who was around. Maybe James got to be a boy of truth from his mom. She was a woman of truth.

It was the morning after Ernest's truck escapade when Ernest said at the breakfast table, "If I had more light I would have been able to handle it."

Ernest's mom looked him in the eye and responded, "What you need to do is get on your knees and thank God for a father who bailed you out."

Mrs. Thorpe was a woman who lived in reality—the reality that we need God. We need His ways. We need His help. That is the truth. And Mrs. Thorpe didn't hold back about it. First thing in the morning in Harrison, Michigan, at the Thorpe's breakfast table, God was crafting life with truth.

8:16 a.m. – Righteousness

Almost simultaneously, in town at the IGA grocery store, Mr. and Mrs. Hansen were getting ready to do their shopping. It had been 52 years of marriage for the Hansen's. Mr. Hansen gently took the hand of his dear wife as he helped

154

her out of the car. She smiled and they walked in together. Here were two people living in forgiveness. You see, life wasn't always like this for the Hansen's. For twenty years Mr. Hansen worked too much, drank too much, and neglected his family too much. He wasn't a bum. He had a good job, was active in the community, and was a regular church attendee. But it wasn't until his wife had a health scare that Mr. Hansen realized what he was doing, and what he wasn't doing. With tears in his eyes he asked for forgiveness. He prayed with his wife that God would change him. That was 32 years ago. God did change him. Now the Hansen's were living proof of righteousness. They were made right with God and each other. They were living out the second chance that Jesus earned on the cross for them. Broken hearts were mended. That's what the righteousness of God does. It protects hearts. At the IGA, God continued to craft life with righteousness.

9:10 a.m. – Readiness

At the Harrison High School track, the cross-country team was doing a morning sprint workout. Pastor Graff was on his way to the funeral home and stopped for a few minutes to watch. He saw the team members flying down the track with their best running shoes on. These boys and girls were confident. They were ready. It was because they knew what was moving them along. Their feet were fitted with the best.

Pastor Graff felt the same way. He wasn't running, however. He was going to bring the Good News of life in Jesus to a family in need. He had prepared and was firmly laced into

155

the gospel of peace. That was his source of confidence. He was ready.

Harrison, Michigan was just one spot where God was crafting life with readiness that came from his Word.

9:36 a.m. – Faith

In the center of town, school registration was in progress. Waiting with her father in line was a young girl by the name of Lee Linn. Lee was unique because she could only get around in a wheelchair. As she and her father waited, another girl made a comment about how different she was.

Lee felt so lonely sometimes. On this day Lee's dad knelt beside her—right there in line—and prayed with her. Lee's father wanted her to know that at every point in life she would need God's doing, His strength, His help, and His leadership. Mr. Linn knew it for himself, too.

Relying on God's doing is called faith. It is a shield of protection in life. God was crafting life with faith inside Lee Linn's heart that day in Harrison, Michigan.

10:05 a.m. – Salvation

It was just after ten o'clock in the morning. Pastor Graff had begun the funeral service he was on his way to earlier in the morning. Mrs. Helen Hoff was 86 years old when she died. Earlier in her life, before her arthritis had sidelined her, she had taught children. Many former students were at the funeral.

156

There was a mixture of tears and joy. But that wasn't the only thing going on.

In heaven there was a scene too amazing to adequately describe. A child of God was being welcomed home. Helen, a servant of Jesus Christ, redeemed by Him, was being ushered into the fullness of life with God. There was a line of people whose lives were touched by Helen. One after another they said, "Welcome" and "Thank you."

Then she heard a warm and wonderful voice. Her Good Shepherd said, "Well done good and faithful servant."

No more arthritis, no more suffering; the time had come for deliverance, release, and salvation. It's what Helen had counted on all along. God was crafting life with salvation on an August morning in Harrison, Michigan.

10:20 a.m. - The Word of God

Back in the funeral home where people gathered for Helen's funeral, God's voice was heard, too. He's not silent when it comes to the lives of His people. People heard the Word of God as Pastor Graff opened his Bible and read words of comfort and life. This was God's voice, speaking up loudly and clearly again, having His say about trouble and grief, offering His help and guidance for life that gets to be too much for anyone to handle. For the ones who still had days on this earth to live, God was crafting life with His Word.

2:20 p.m. – Life's Essentials

Over the summer Mrs. Thorpe was able to get a few rounds of golf in with her daughter Karen. Both Karen and her mom noticed that the hazards kept getting tougher. On the third hole of their favorite course there used to be a farmer with a trap door under him. But they painted over him and put an alien there. It's hard to get the ball through that little trap door! That's one of the unique challenges of miniature golf.

The most challenging hole in miniature golf is the last one. It may not be tough to play, but it's not easy to say goodbye to your golf ball, is it? Once you put the ball in the hole, the ball is gone. That's the hole Karen always made her mom go first on.

That's the way miniature golf is. That's the way life is too. It's going to come to an end. You might not think about it. You might try to deny it. But one day it will be over.

Each day passes like that. That's why God urges all of us to be ready for life. He calls us to approach each day as craftsmen. If we wear the full set of armor He gives, if we use all the tools He provides, then we will have accomplished the craftsmanship task of living He intends for our lives. And we'll have something to show for it.

In just one day in Harrison, Michigan, God was coming through. In small ways He was providing what was truly important in life. He was giving everything needed for a strong life, a life crafted by Him.

158

8:30 p.m. – Prayer

Later that evening, back at the Thorpe home, Mr. Thorpe knelt at the bedsides of his children to say bedtime prayers. Every chance he got he brought his own life and the lives of his children before the Lord in prayer. There would be no closing of the eyes without first asking God to keep His eyes open. Prayer is essential because life is not supposed to be just closed-eyed complacency. It is meant to be a vigilant journey with God. As the day ended in Harrison, God was crafting life with prayer.

Being Strong

> *"Stand firm then, with the belt of truth buckled around your waist, with the breastplate of righteousness in place, and with your feet fitted with the readiness that comes from the gospel of peace. In addition to all this, take up the shield of faith, with which you can extinguish all the flaming arrows of the evil one. Take the helmet of salvation and the sword of the Spirit, which is the word of God. And pray in the Spirit on all occasions with all kinds of prayers and requests. With this in mind, be alert and always keep on praying for all the saints"* (Ephesians 6:14-18).

That's a life crafted by the Lord Jesus Christ and His Spirit. That is a life that is strong—each and every day.

Devotion/Study Guide for chapter 20: Being Strong

Discuss:

Read Ephesians 6:10-20

What part of the day in Harrison connects with your life most?

How do you see God putting life-essentials in your life?

Apply:

Talk about each piece of armor and how it fits into your life today.

Pray:

Thank God for giving you what you need in life. Ask Him about one or two pieces of armor that you especially need for your life lately.

Becoming Whole
A Time for Joy
Chapter Twenty-one

———————————

"Rejoice in the Lord always. I will say it again: Rejoice!"
Philippians 4:4

School years go quickly and slowly. Days that are filled with assignments and activities fly by. Kids grow before your eyes. But sometimes the pace seems like it has slowed to a standstill. When you're on math problem thirty-eight with ten more to go at ten-o'clock at night, the pace is agonizingly slow. When you've reached November and the days are cold and snowy, when nobody can play outside, and when people are getting sick and cranky, the school year seems to take forever.

That's when the challenges of family life seem to rise to a crescendo as well.

Ernest's senior year in high school was going well. There were no big problems at the moment. He was pretty independent and actually helped with all the errands and chauffeuring that had to be done.

Karen needed a little more time and attention, especially with all her school assignments. Mrs. Thorpe was the number one homework helper. She could handle the complexities of the human nervous system and the details of how nutrients entered the soil of the rainforest, but it was an extra challenge to navigate through those subjects while three-year-old James pulled on her sleeve and insisted on giving her the latest update on the cartoon he was watching.

James was a handful. During the dreary days of November, he was a leading cause for Mrs. Thorpe to feel the anxieties of life.

Since her husband got his job back he had been away from home with more overtime than ever. This was good for the financial picture, but it was another drastic change at home. For the past year Mrs. Thorpe had been working and her husband had been home. Now she was carrying the load on the home front. And she didn't feel like she was getting anywhere.

Oh, there were attempts to break the routine and get refreshed. Mrs. Thorpe decided to go to McDonald's for lunch one day when the sun finally peeked through the northern Michigan overcast. Ernest and Karen were in school. It would be a happy mother and son outing, just James and his mom. But then everything broke loose.

You have to understand that James had an aversion to pickles. He couldn't stand them. Typically this was not a problem. Mrs. Thorpe kept James out of certain grocery store aisles. She kept the pickles out of sight at home—no one was a big fan of them anyway.

As Mrs. Thorpe placed her order she was very careful to instruct the person waiting on her to make sure the hamburger Happy Meal had a PLAIN hamburger in it—nothing on it. Mrs. Thorpe carried the food over to the table as James followed happily behind. On this unusually wonderful and sunny November day, the last thing Mrs. Thorpe expected to encounter was PICKLES.

After they prayed a prayer of thanks together, Mrs. Thorpe and James began to eat. James opened his mouth and took a big bite of his hamburger. Pickles! There were pickles on his plain hamburger! He not only saw the pickles; he tasted them! Even the people outside in the drive-through line could hear the screams. Mrs. Thorpe helped him get the pickles out of his mouth, but the screams were full power and not letting up.

Right at that moment in McDonald's a group of twelve ladies from the Congregational Church just began their monthly Bible Breakfast lesson (How the breakfast turned into a lunch is another story!). Mrs. Thorpe felt the look of twenty-four eyes that seemed to say, "Can't you control your child?" Mrs. Thorpe felt like telling them, "It's the pickles! It's the pickles!" But she didn't want rumors of her insanity circulating around town. No, all she could do was bail out. She packed up, picked up James, and left the restaurant as quickly as she could. The screaming and crying filled her van as she drove away.

Mrs. Thorpe's heart was heavy on the way home. "It's supposed to be the most wonderful time of the year," she thought, "So why do I feel so terrible?"

When they returned home Mrs. Thorpe collapsed on the couch. Her head was pounding. Maybe just a little rest would help. Unfortunately James took that opportunity to find his sister's scented markers and color his Elmo sheets. Mrs. Thorpe wondered how much more she could take.

By the time Sunday came, Mrs. Thorpe was at a low ebb in the level of any joy in her life. The whole family was visiting Mr. and Mrs. Thorpe's nephew's church that Sunday. Their nephew was reading a Scripture lesson for the first time and they all wanted to support him and celebrate the day. Between passing Cheerios and raisins to James, Mrs. Thorpe heard the pastor read from Luke chapter twenty-one: *"On the earth nations will be in anguish and perplexity at the roaring and tossing of the sea. Men will faint from terror, apprehensive of what is coming on the world...Be careful, or your hearts will be weighed down with...the anxieties of life" (vss. 25, 26, 34).* She thought to herself, "Can I ever relate to that!"

Heaviness of heart, anguish, perplexity, the anxieties of life—they're all part of what you go through in this world separated from God. And they can be overwhelming. Life that is weighed down with sin never fails to drain the joy right out of you.

Then Mrs. Thorpe heard a tearing sound. Oh, no! It was a hymnal! Mrs. Thorpe didn't intend to scream audibly, but she couldn't help it. Her gasp and her quick action to separate James from the now damaged hymnal scared James and caused him to start crying. All Mrs. Thorpe could think about was the McDonald's episode. She scooped up James and made a quick retreat to the lobby. She sat James down so she could pick up the supplies that fell out of her purse, and that's when James started to take his clothes off. Mrs. Thorpe intervened and picked James up to try to calm him down. He was heavy. She was doing the "back of the church rock"—that desperate swaying motion that parents of young children know so well. This was not turning out to be a worshipful day!

Finally Mr. Thorpe left Ernest and Karen, took James from his mother's tired arms, and walked off in the direction of the bathroom. All Mrs. Thorpe could do was sit down and cry. She sat with her head in her hands. That was it. She was waving the white flag. She had nothing left.

> *"You know, dear, the Lord will get you through this. He'll help you be just fine."*

At that very moment Mrs. Thorpe felt an arm around her shoulder. She looked up and sitting beside her was a woman she didn't even know. The woman was in her sixties. She was wearing a choir robe. All she did was give Mrs. Thorpe a hug and say, "You know, dear, the Lord will get you through this. He'll help you be just fine."

Mrs. Thorpe couldn't even reply. All she could do was cry and be grateful for someone who was taking some of the anxiety away, someone who was bringing her joy.

While Mrs. Thorpe sat with her eyes closed, embraced by a comforter and new friend, she heard her nephew read these

165

words from the Bible: *"May the Lord make your love increase and overflow for each other and for everyone else, just as ours does for you. May he strengthen your hearts so that you will be blameless and holy in the presence of our God and Father when our Lord Jesus comes with all his holy ones"(1 Thess. 3:12-13).*

That day in church Mrs. Thorpe heard that because of His love for us Jesus came for the anxieties of life. She saw Him come close in the love and care of a woman who reached out to her in her distress. Later He came close again when Mrs. Thorpe stood at the altar for communion. Jesus knew that the last days would be tough—that life would weigh hearts down. And for those tough times Jesus said, *"When these things begin to take place, stand up and lift up your heads, because your redemption is drawing near" (Luke 21:28).* He was talking about Himself. Jesus drew near.

Isaiah 53 says, *"Surely he has borne our griefs and carried our sorrows."* The anxieties of life are not ours alone to bear. Jesus carried all anxiety and all heaviness of heart to the cross. He left all of it nailed there and arose from death to bring a new heart and new spirit to people in need, to people like Mrs. Thorpe during the dreary days of November. She saw in a vivid way, at just the right time, that in times of anxiety, Jesus brings needed JOY.

Devotion/Study Guide for chapter 21: A Time for Joy

Discuss:

Read John 15:9-11

What was a primary purpose for Jesus' coming?

How did Mrs. Thorpe see this work of Jesus in her life?

How does Jesus bring His joy to your life?

Read Psalm 51:10-12

What causes you to lose your joy in life? How does God restore it?

Apply:

Read Psalm 94:16-19

What anxiety are you experiencing right now? What comfort do these verses bring?

Pray:

Thank Jesus for a time He brought joy into your distress. Ask Him to help you in one distressed area of your life.

A Time for Wholeness
Chapter Twenty-two

"Every valley shall be filled in, every mountain and hill made low. The crooked roads shall become straight, the rough ways smooth. And all mankind will see God's salvation." Luke 3:5-6

N ow wait just one minute. How can I start another chapter when there is an unresolved issue in the last chapter? You might remember that I mentioned the Bible breakfast that the ladies from the Congregational Church had every week at the McDonald's in Harrison. The gathering started as a breakfast, but it turned into a lunch. I can't leave you hanging, so here's the story of what happened.

A group of ladies from the Congregational Church in town decided to meet every Thursday morning at 7:45 for study of the Bible, prayer together, and encouragement of one another. It was a good plan and a worthy activity. McDonald's was a morning hot-spot in Harrison, so the ladies figured they would be a good witness, too. Perhaps some people they met would even join their group.

So, each Thursday morning each member of the group got up a little earlier than usual, got ready, finished some tasks at home, and met at McDonald's by 7:45.

Their routine started in September. Everything was going smoothly until the week after Thanksgiving. That week, some group members seemed a little distracted. People straggled in late. The leader of the group, Grace Mittvoke, asked everyone if it was okay to continue meeting with the holidays coming up. Everybody said yes. In fact, the group took pride in staying on schedule. They set their goals and accomplished what they set out to do. The group was not only dedicated. They were driven. The plan would work. No matter what it took the plan would work. These folks were not quitters. They were from hardy stock. Even if it was a challenge, they made a promise to God Himself! They were not going to let Him down.

So Grace said, "Let the study begin!"

But the following week the group ran into a few glitches. Kiersten Protem brought some papers with her from the office. "I just wanted to put a dent in the pile before I go into work," she said. "Things are really hectic. We're getting so much stuff. And this is the new paperless system!" Kiersten thought she could sort through her collection of memos and mail while people were finishing off their pancakes.

Another member of the group asked if it would be all right if she came just a half hour late. Mrs. Nystrom was caring for her husband at home. He had surgery not too long ago and now needed a few things done before she could get out of the house. Mrs. Nystrom was so tired that it was getting hard to get up extra early.

Then Janice Wallace chimed in. She would get the kids off to school, but with trying to decorate for Christmas, the beds were not getting made and, after homework and post-school snacks, she was ending up doing the breakfast dishes at suppertime.

At that point everybody saw Lydia Carrier struggling with something in the booth area she was in. She confessed. She snuck a couple of strands of Christmas lights in her purse to untangle them during any down times in the Bible study. She even had her bulb tester with her!

What was going on? Everyone seemed to be overwhelmed! And as the Bible class group members talked about how overwhelmed they felt, they saw Grace pick up her cross-stitch. "It's a Christmas gift that HAS to get done," she said.

When Viola Johnson's cell phone rang, that was it. Something had to be done! They were getting together to study God's Word, but too much was getting in the way even to hear Him.

The group happened to be studying the Christmas accounts in the Bible. They were on John the Baptist. As the group pondered their overwhelmed feeling, Grace said, "Wait a minute. What did we read for today?" She turned to Luke chapter three and read these words, *"Prepare the way for the Lord, make straight paths for him. Every valley shall be filled in, every mountain and hill made low. The crooked roads shall become straight, the rough ways smooth. And all mankind will see God's salvation."*

Grace said, "Why don't we do what John said? Why don't we prepare the way for Jesus? Let's clear all these things away and come ready to meet our Savior, otherwise we'll miss Him."

> *They asked Jesus to lead them, to create a straight path for Him into their hearts and lives.*

Then Viola Johnson put her now deactivated cell phone on the table and said, "Why don't we pray for the Lord's guidance right now?"

Lydia stuffed the Christmas lights back into her purse. "Yes," she said, "let's pray."

So they did. They asked Jesus to lead them, to create a straight path for Him into their hearts and lives. They asked that their study of the Word would fill their valleys, would remove the obstacles in their lives, and would smooth out the rough roads of life they were on. They were depending on Jesus for this. And that day in McDonald's they lifted up their lives to Him again. The Holy Spirit was returning them to their Savior from places that were in disrepair and far away.

That's what repentance is. Do you face any crooked roads these days? You know how it is—there's too much to do. You're trying to get caught up. You feel overwhelmed! Do you

172

have any mountains or hills in your life—barriers of too much happening in your life physically or emotionally? And what about the valleys? Illness, grief, depression, hard times? John said: *"Every valley shall be **filled in**, every mountain and hill **made low**. The crooked roads shall **become straight**, the rough ways **smooth**. And all mankind **will see God's salvation**."*

How does that happen? How does Jesus fill in the valleys, make the mountains low, straighten out the roads and smooth out the rough going? The ladies at the Bible Breakfast began to see it all very clearly. It was just like Psalm 23 says, *"Even though I walk through the valley of the shadow of death, you are with me."*

It was just as Jesus said—that by faith, God doing His doing in life, even a mountain can be moved into the middle of the sea. It was just the way Jesus declared for rough and crooked times, *"Come to me all you who are weary and burdened and I will give you rest" (Matthew 11:28).*

From all their busyness those ladies were brought back to their Savior who gave His life on the cross, who delivered them from sin and the valley of death, who straightened the road between them and God by forgiving their sins and giving them the gift of eternal life. He was even with them in McDonald's. There wasn't any valley too deep or mountain too high or road too rough or crooked for Him to take care of.

Jesus was calling out to them, "Here I am. Watch me. Trust me. Turn to me. I am your Savior."

173

That's what the Bible Breakfast group in Harrison did. They changed. They agreed to prepare before they came. They were going to get everything out of the way before they arrived. When they stepped into McDonald's they would be ready for God's Word to come into their lives and make them whole again. So they moved their breakfast to lunch. They put a clock in the middle of the table. On the clock was a special reminder, an engraving that read, "Time is grace." Each time they got together, do you know what they saw? Through all the valleys and mountains and crooked and rough roads, they saw God's salvation. They saw His love and help.

When they saw Mrs. Thorpe with her pickle-shocked son in McDonald's that fateful day, their look was not saying, "Can't you control your son?" It was saying "We remember those days."

That very moment they prayed for the poor woman who looked so distressed and ran out of the restaurant. They prayed that Jesus would help her during this overwhelming time. They prayed that she would be made whole.

Devotion/Study Guide for chapter 22: A Time for Wholeness

Discuss:

Read 2 Peter 3:8-9

What do these verses say about time? What new perspective do they give you?

The ladies in the Bible breakfast experienced a "paradigm shift." What opportunities to change do you have in your life because of God's patience?

Read Philippians 4:4-9

What are the "valleys" in your life right now? How do these verses help fill them in?

Apply:

Read Colossians 3:1-10

How do these verses straighten any "crooked roads" you might be on right now? What changes do you need to make in your life that will correct your actions that may be destructive to yourself and others?

Pray:

Ask the Holy Spirit to lead you to repentance in an area of life that needs to change. Thank God for the gift of a new beginning.

Becoming Whole
A Time for Changes
Chapter Twenty-three

"John exhorted the people and preached the good news to them." Luke 3:18

E rnest Thorpe was thoroughly enjoying his senior year at Harrison High School. He was also enjoying his independence. Ernest was getting out, doing his thing, driving around, participating in after school activities, and soaking in every minute of this grand finale year in Harrison. Part of his fairly new independence was his special plan for Christmas shopping. Ernest wanted to drive to Bay City. There was a nice mall there. It had a much bigger selection than he could ever find in Harrison. He wanted that expanded selection because of his desire to pick out something special for the members of his family—and for the girl he was going out with. So he talked to his parents about taking the trip the following Saturday. They agreed, and the excursion was on!

When some of the kids at school found out that Ernest was going to Bay City, they approached him during the week with a plan. They said, "Hey Ernest, we'll pay for the gas if you take us along. We'll tell our parents that we're at each other's houses; you drop us off in Bay City so we can do what we want; then pick us up and they'll never know the difference."

It didn't take long for Ernest to reply. "Forget it!" he said.

As he walked away he could hear them grumbling and making remarks about him just because they couldn't have their way. "Bad news," Ernest thought.

Saturday came quickly and Ernest set out for Bay City. He had Christmas music playing in the car and was looking forward to finding the gifts that were just right. As he neared his destination, traffic started to get a little thick. Ahead of him in the left lane Ernest saw a truck full of chickens. Ernest had to slow down and was watching to see whether or not the chicken truck would move over to the right. At that moment a Camaro came up quickly behind Ernest. Before Ernest could do anything, the driver behind him started flashing her lights and laying on the horn. Then, just as quickly, she swerved into the right lane and blew by Ernest. As she passed by, Ernest could see the driver yelling all kinds of things at him. The driver had that twisted kind of angry face drivers get when they lose control. Ernest thought, "Whew, there's some road rage. I'm staying behind the chickens."

Ernest got off the expressway and had to separate from his chicken truck escort a couple of blocks before the mall. He was getting back into the Christmas spirit about the time he pulled into the parking lot. It was crowded, so he cruised the aisles to find a space. He didn't really care if he had a spot close

178

or far away. Walking was good for him and there were plenty of people who needed a close spot. Ernest found one of the few available spots and was just about to pull in when a car sped around him and took the spot! It was the Camaro from the highway! The driver got out and hustled her two kids toward the mall. She didn't even look at Ernest. It was heads down, every person for himself, into the mall.

"It's a jungle out here," Ernest thought. But this was not going to ruin his shopping expedition. He parked across the street by a movie theater and hiked to his destination.

> *"It's a jungle out here," Ernest thought. But this was not going to ruin his shopping expedition.*

The mall was packed with people. Ernest was not a big fan of crowds, but he had a special mission. So, onward he went through the mall. He paused at an electronics store. There were some TV's in the window with good basketball games on. Ernest stood with a crowd of package and coat-laden men. The seventy-two inch big screen showed a player berating his coach. The coach made a decision that the player didn't agree with.

"It's everywhere," Ernest thought. "Hey, I know the driver of a Camaro you might like to meet."

The shopping day was successful for Ernest. He found the gifts he wanted to purchase. The last one to buy was for his mom. She had worked hard all year and Ernest wanted to get her something special. He went into a nice store to find the right thing for her. Ernest had been working and had some money to spend. As he was in the store he noticed that he had a partner. Every time he went down an aisle, a man who was trying to look nonchalant followed him. Perfume section? There he was. Gloves and scarves? There he was again. It was security. Ernest knew it was necessary, but he did a couple of laps around the underwear section just for fun.

Ernest purchased the gift from a cashier who did not look at him once or speak to him. He wished her a merry Christmas and left the store with the present he found for his mom. As he left he heard the security person say into his two-way radio, "High schooler's gone. It's clear."

Ernest shook his head in disbelief. As he left the mall he said, "Houston, we've got a problem." It was time to go home.

When he arrived back home he concealed his presents and sat down by his dad.

"How'd it go, son?" Ernest's dad asked.

"Dad," Ernest replied, "I've got some bad news for you. We live in a crabby world."

That's what the selfishness, anger, impatience, unfriendliness, bullying, and lack of contentment added up to. It was bad news. Ernest wondered where the good news went during Christmas. He was happy about his purchases, but he was disillusioned about his Christmas shopping experience.

"I'm ready for some good news," Ernest thought as he lay down to go to sleep.

Sunday morning arrived along with the Thorpe family's trek to St. Luke Lutheran for church. Pastor Graff preached on John the Baptist in Luke chapter three. Crowds of people were coming out to John. Maybe it was like the mall at Christmas. But John wasn't letting these people stay in their crabbiness. He said, *"Produce fruit in keeping with repentance."* It was time for changes—life changes.

John said, *"I'm baptizing you here in the river. The main character in this drama, to whom I'm a mere stagehand, will ignite the kingdom of life, a fire, the Holy Spirit within you, changing you from the inside out. He's going to clean house— make a clean sweep of your lives. He'll place everything in its true and proper place before God; everything false he'll put out with the trash to be burned"* (Luke 3:16-18, The Message).

When Ernest heard those words, Christmas made a lot more sense to him. What a difference between what God does and what we do! Ernest saw a lot missing on Saturday. Today he saw that Jesus brings everything we need.

Beneath the pretty decorations and the gentle songs of Christmas, Ernest was exposed to the crabby world. He knew that he was part of that crabby world, too. All of us are. And all of us need a change.

That's what Jesus came to do. Beneath the peace and joy of the little baby Jesus born in Bethlehem was the raging of

181

sin, strife, terror and corruption. Jesus came to make a clean sweep of all that. He faced a world of mall rudeness, road rage and more as He hung on the cross. And through His death and resurrection He changed it all. He cleaned house! The risen Lord burned the trash of sin and opened his hand to give us all new life and a new approach to living!

Pastor Graff quoted Luke 3 again, *"With many other words John exhorted the people and preached the good news to them."*

Good news! There it was—exactly what Ernest was looking for.

These were good times and bad times for Ernest Thorpe. Because of his dad's job loss for a year, Ernest's college option was questionable. He felt some worry and disappointment as he faced the future. There was a lot of uncertainty in his life. But if any changes were going to happen, Ernest would gladly take the ones that Jesus handed out.

Devotion/Study Guide for chapter 23: A Time for Changes

Discuss:

Read Matthew 24:10-13

What do these verses say about the "coldness" you might experience in life?

This week, how have you experienced the world's crabbiness like Ernest did? What is the cause?

What do you need to oppose it and to stand firm?

Read James 2:8-13

How do these verses lead you to live a life of mercy? How can you be merciful?

Apply:

Read James 2:14-17

How do these verses lead you to a life of action in this world? What actions can you do to show that your faith is alive?

Pray:

Ask God to make you a person who brings His Good News to the people around you. Thank Him for one way His Good News makes your life better.

Becoming Whole
A Time to Believe
Chapter Twenty-four

"Sing to the LORD a new song; sing to the LORD, all the earth." Psalm 96:1

E rnest Thorpe was not ready to sing. In addition to his participation in cross-country, track, the school newspaper and a few other school activities, Ernest Thorpe also sang in the Harrison High School Chorus. The chorus wasn't the most popular activity at school. In fact, the numbers were at an all time low during Ernest's senior year. People just didn't want to sing. Ernest didn't know why. But he did know that the chorus was not ready for its holiday concert! It was coming the Friday night before Christmas—way too soon for a group that just wasn't singing. Rehearsals were terrible. The director of the chorus was a part time musician who claimed to have directed a Salvation Army band at one time. He was a virtual volunteer and, in view of the student participation level, the price was right for the school administration. So Ernest tried to get through rehearsal. The director sat at the piano with his face hidden behind sheet music. Nobody in the chorus could tell whether he was giving hand cues to sections or smoothing out the perpetual twang in his hair.

To complicate matters, the wrestling coach was the faculty advisor to the chorus. Ernest would not have made that casting move. The wrestling coach just didn't fit the Pavarotti kind of image. He didn't even fit the seven dwarfs "whistle while you work" image. He just didn't sing! With a newspaper laid out on the desk, the wrestling coach faked that he was paying attention to rehearsal while he was catching up on the news of the day.

As another disaster of a rehearsal finished up Ernest walked out of the music room thinking, "We're going to be terrible. We are terrible. We need help."

That's when he ran into Paul Tucker.

"Hey Paul," Ernest said desperate for some musical reinforcement, "we need you in the chorus. Why don't you join? I've heard you humming around the hallways a little bit. You've got a good voice. What do you think?"

Paul looked at Ernest with disbelief. "No way," he said. "Do you think you're going to get ME to sing? It's not going to happen. Why would I want to sing? Why, Ernest? Why sing?"

Paul avoided the music room as he left for home.

Why sing? That was a good question.

Ernest went home. He walked in the door and said to his mom, "Nobody sings anymore, mom."

"Tough rehearsal Ernest?" his mom replied.

"Oh yeah," said Ernest.

Ernest sat down and turned the television on. Why sing? Why sing? Not because of the news reports he was seeing on TV.

Why sing? Not because people are always very kind.

Why sing? Not because all the problems in the world are solved or improving.

Why sing? Not because you always feel so great inside.

Why sing? Not because Ernest was so sure about college anymore—there was not going to be enough money for him to go next year.

Why sing? Ernest walked down the hallway toward his bedroom and heard James screaming as his mom clipped his fingernails. Definitely not a reason to sing.

Why sing? Because you got your list of things to do finished? Because you're proud of personal accomplishments?

Why sing? Why sing—when you've been through so much in life and you wonder how much more of it you can take?

Why sing?

Why sing in a world broken and sinful?

Why sing when you are faced with personal doubts and tough issues?

Why sing when you are tired and sad?

Common sense says that there are so many reasons NOT to sing. Ernest saw that.

On Wednesday evening the Thorpe family attended a special Advent worship service. It was a memorial service to remember and give thanks to God for loved ones who had died through the years. This had become a special and comforting tradition at St. Luke Lutheran Church. Christmas time was when people seemed to feel their grief the most, so Pastor Graff set aside the last Advent Wednesday to gather together and receive the comfort of Jesus, the One who conquered death. It was a great time of focus for so many people in the community. And it was a great time to proclaim the real reason for Christmas, a Savior born to us, Jesus Christ.

Common sense says that there are so many reasons NOT to sing. Ernest saw that.

The worship service ended with the singing of "Joy to the World." The congregation stood and sang out. Ernest heard a strong and wonderful voice behind him. He turned around as they sang the line "and wonders of His love." It was the WRESTLING COACH! He was singing! He was singing! He nodded and smiled at Ernest as they finished up the song.

Why was he singing? He must have had a reason. Ernest thought about Mary from the reading they heard that evening from Luke chapter one.

Mary sang, too. Why did she sing? Was it because she had a pretty voice? No.

Was it because life was going wonderfully for her? No.

Was it because she felt strong and fearless? No.

Was it because it made sense to sing? Not at all.

Young, frightened and uncertain Mary described the reasons for her singing in the words of her song. *"My spirit rejoices in God my Savior,"* she sang. *"The Mighty One has done great things for me...His mercy extends to those who fear him...He has filled the hungry with good things...He has helped his servant..."*

That's why Mary sang—because of God's amazing work, because of the Savior Jesus. That's why she sang. Against all sense and observation, she had a reason to sing.

That's why the wrestling coach was singing. He was holding on to the news of eternal life in Jesus Christ for His life and for someone he loved. He had a reason to sing.

Elizabeth said to Mary, *"Blessed is she who has believed that what the Lord has said to her will be accomplished!"* Mary believed. When everything seemed to be going wrong, her Lord and Savior was the one she could trust.

Friday night came. The Harrison High School Chorus performed for their holiday concert. Ernest sang! The closing number was "Joy to the World," and Ernest sang out. The choir director was even distracted from his sheet music by all that singing. Ernest knew why he could sing. He had a reason.

Ernest came home singing that night. The next day he would see what was stuffed in the mailbox—a thick manila envelope with a University of Michigan track team return address. There was no doubt: God would keep doing His amazing work. For now, Ernest was just glad to sing about it.

Devotion/Study Guide for chapter 24: A Time to Believe

Discuss:

Read Psalm 33:1-5

Why does God's Word give you a reason to sing?

What new outlook and attitude does God's Word cause in you?

Read Ephesians 5:15-20

How does the new song God gives you show in your relationships with others?

How do these verses help lead you to show the love of Jesus?

Apply:

Read Psalm 13:1-6

You may know someone who has a lot of sadness in his or her life. What answer for sorrow do these verses bring? How can you communicate this truth to the people you know who are in need?

Pray:

Thank God for one reason He has given you to sing.

Conclusion
More Steps Forward
Chapter Twenty-five

"The plans of the righteous are just, but the advice of the wicked is deceitful." Proverbs 12:5

T he envelope. What was in the envelope?

Ernest Thorpe may have been a singer, but he wasn't a dancer. You should have seen him dance, however, when he opened up that University of Michigan envelope and found that he was being given a full-ride track scholarship to the University of Michigan!

It was more than he could have ever asked for or imagined.

Ernest had to be one of the happiest freshmen at the University. In fact, he was loving every minute of his college experience. Life at the University of Michigan in Ann Arbor was exciting, interesting, stimulating and fun. When he started college he looked at the surface attractions of college life—more girls than he had ever seen in his entire life in Harrison! But now he was more experienced and he moved into appreciating the subtle benefits of the university experience—an amazing number of late night parties!

Ernest discovered that a bunch of guys gathered together every Friday night for what they called "Friday Late Night." At about two in the morning they would meet in a selected dorm room to talk, relax, laugh and be college guys. Some of Ernest's friends invited him, so he went along.

That was the first time Ernest heard the phrase "do a hogback." Yes, it sounds strange, but Ernest found out that some of these Friday Late Night attendees had a new-school-year tradition. Hogback referred to Hogback Road, a fairly remote road on the outskirts of Ann Arbor. "Doing a Hogback" involved climbing into the back of a pickup truck that one of the guys owned, and speeding backwards down Hogback Road in the wee hours of the morning. The group laughed about the hills and being thrown around in the back of the pickup truck. Ernest couldn't believe what he was hearing. This was dangerous and insane. This went against everything he was taught. It was against the law! This could kill people. And then he was invited to go along.

What a strange situation he was in. This was something he would never even think about doing, never even consider, never even dream up. But here he was at Friday Late Night with friends. And he was considering it! He heard statements like,

"C'mon, we do it every year!"

"This is tradition!"

"Yeah, it's a little risky; it doesn't exactly follow the rules of the road, but this is different."

"It's college; we have the right to have some fun."

194

In a strange way, all that input was starting to make sense to him. Maybe they were right. He didn't think so, but what did he know? Fortunately the Friday Late Night got too late and ended. Ernest went back to his room with the invitation to "do a hogback" still waiting for a reply.

The next morning, a little too early, Ernest had to get up and meet his hometown friend and mentor, Manny Andrews. Manny had come down to go on a training run with Ernest. Manny was still the best runner ever to come out of Harrison. He could also still beat Ernest easily. As they ran, Ernest told Manny about the "hogback" conversation.

Manny replied, "They're doing a Daniel on you."

"A what?" Ernest asked.

"A Daniel," Manny answered. "You remember in Daniel when the advisers got together and gave the king bad advice. They said that everybody agreed about the law of worshipping and praying to the king alone. They advised the king to make the law, and they guaranteed it would be a great thing. Remember that?"

Ernest said, "Yeah, I do."

"So what happened when the king took bad advice?" Manny asked.

Ernest told the story, "Daniel got tossed to the lions and the king totally regretted his decision."

"Exactly," Manny said. "You follow bad advice and it ends in big time hurt and regret."

"But it's hard being on the outside," Ernest said.

"Yeah it's hard," Manny replicd. "It's called suffering. It's called suffering for what is right. And that's life when you don't buy bad advice. But, who knows, maybe you'll even turn the tables and give some good advice in the process."

Manny was the old guy—over forty now. But he had been a reliable person in Ernest's life since high school. Manny described the bad advice that hits all of us: TV advice that portrays wrong actions as normal, groups of friends who get lots of courage to steer you the wrong direction, statements that are easy to make around the water cooler or at lunch with co-workers, but bring destruction in life:

"Why don't you just leave her?"

"One stop at the bar before you go home won't hurt anyone."

"It's just innocent flirting."

"Who's gonna know?"

"You should get revenge."

"You have the right to do what you want."

Manny talked about advice from hurtful people who say:

"You'll never change."

"There's no hope for you."

"You've got no future."

"Who are you to think that you'll ever be anything?"

Manny talked about the way the devil and our own blind selves spout bad advice:

"You're fine on your own."

"What difference can God make—He's boring and irrelevant."

"Let your kids figure out spirituality for themselves."

"Do good things and be happy and your life will be complete."

All of it was bad advice.

Manny said, "Why believe a lie, Ernest? Why bet your life on bad advice? I guarantee that regret will come out of that situation. Go with the good advice in Daniel and see where that leads."

It was a good run, a good talk, and food for thought. Ernest decided to take a look at Daniel. He did just that the following Friday. Late. In his own room. He read the bad advice of the administrators. He heard their generalizations, their flattery and their pressure. He saw how the crowd-mentality sounded so good, but led to some destructive acts. Then he read Daniel 6:23, *"The king was overjoyed and ordered that Daniel be lifted from the den. Not a scratch was found on him because he had trusted in his God."*

Manny didn't come out and say it, but Ernest discovered the source of good advice. "He had trusted in his God." That was the standard. That was the truth among so many lies. Then Ernest read how the king destroyed the troublemakers.

"Keep bad advice at a distance, and good advice close by," Ernest thought. "Like staying away from Friday Late Night."

The next morning one of his friends woke him up too early again. There was some bad news. A pickup truck with some students in it rolled over on Hogback Road early that morning. One was airlifted to a Detroit hospital. The driver was okay, but was really shaken up. The seriously injured kid was the driver's little brother.

"Regrets." Ernest heard Manny Andrews' words echo in his mind. "I guarantee that regret will come out of that situation." Ernest said a prayer to himself.

There is a lot of bad advice in life. It comes from inside yourself. It comes at you from the people and world around you. But there is some good advice. It is what King Darius discovered after the lion's den debacle. He summed it up in His message to the world (vss. 25-27), *"Peace and prosperity to you! I decree that everyone throughout my kingdom should tremble with fear before the God of Daniel. For he is the living God, and he will endure forever. His kingdom will never be destroyed, and his rule will never end. He rescues and saves his people; he performs miraculous signs and wonders in the heavens and on earth. He has rescued Daniel from the power of the lions."*

God wants you to have good advice. He allowed Daniel to go through the lion's den experience so the king could have it. He sent His only Son, Jesus, to suffer, die, and rise again, so you could have that good advice, too. It is the counsel that your life is precious, that you have a refuge and strength, that you aren't in this all alone, and that you have a home in heaven when you die.

God let Ernest wrestle with "doing a Hogback" so he could get some good advice, too—words of life from a trusted friend.

What advice are you following? Ernest Thorpe was determined to listen to the right voice so he could keep taking more steps forward. Why go in any other direction?

Devotion/Study Guide for chapter 25: More Steps Forward

Discuss:

Read Philippians 2:12-16

What pressures did Ernest feel at "Friday Late Night"?

How does the wisdom Manny shared relate to your life today?

What challenges are you facing when it comes to "working out your salvation"?

Apply:

Think of one way you will "shine like stars in the universe as you hold out the word of life" this week.

Pray:

Ask God to keep giving you steps forward in your faith. Ask for courage to go against the pressure of conformity in one area of your life. Ask God to use you as a tool to give His good advice.

Acknowledgements

I am so thankful to the Lord Jesus that He has allowed me to share His Word of truth through stories. Jesus' parables drew people in, were relevant to their lives, and brought home a powerful message. My prayer is that the Lord uses the stories in this book to surprise you, to cause you to think, to stir your heart, to encourage you in your faith, and to redirect your steps as you follow Jesus.

In order to spin these yarns well, I needed a lot of help. First, I want to thank my wife who became my chief editor as she gave this book a test run. Her encouragement, laughter, and hard work are evidence of her abiding and Christ-like love. I praise God for her!

I would also like to thank both my daughters, Hannah and Abby, for listening to all the stories I told them over the years. They were always eager to hear one more. Hannah became my final proofreader, too. I am grateful for her time and talent.

Prince of Peace Lutheran Church is where Ernest first appeared on the scene. The dear people there listened graciously and gave me loads of encouragement to keep them up to date about Ernest and his exploits. I am deeply grateful for the time they gave me to complete this second volume of "Ernest stories."

Finally, I want to thank you, the reader of this book. I pray you are blessed, and I pray you spread the word!

Michael W. Newman

About the Author

Michael Newman has been a pastor, teacher, author, and speaker for over 20 years. He has served churches in Texas, Minnesota, and in the Chicago area, and continues to be active in writing, and in a variety of preaching and teaching venues. Married to his wife Cindy since 1983, they have been blessed with two wonderful daughters. When not preaching and teaching, you might catch him hanging out with his family, running a few miles on the Texas roads, risking his life doing yard work, or enjoying a good book.

More books written by Michael W. Newman:

Harrison Town

Satan's Lies

To find more resources and information, go to
www.ABCPassages.com.

To take a look at and purchase books, search "Michael W. Newman" at Amazon.com.